CONFIGURING PRODUCT INFORMATION MANAGEMENT WITHIN DYNAMICS 365 FOR OPERATIONS

MODULE 1: CONFIGURING THE PRODUCT INFORMATION MANAGEMENT CONTROLS

Murray Fife

ISBN-13: 978-1979498456

ISBN-10: 1979498458

Preface

What You Need for this Guide

All the examples shown in this blueprint were done with the Microsoft Dynamics 365 for Operations hosted image that was provisioned through Lifecycle Services.

The following list of software from the virtual image was leveraged within this guide:

Microsoft Dynamics 365 for Operations

Even though all the preceding software was used during the development and testing of the recipes in this book, they should also work on later versions without any changes.

Errata

Although we have taken every care to ensure the accuracy of our content, mistakes do happen. If you find a mistake in one of our books—maybe a mistake in the text or the code—we would be grateful if you would report this to us. By doing so, you can save other readers from frustration and help us improve subsequent versions of this book. If you find any errata, please report them by emailing editor@dynamicscompanions.com.

Piracy

Piracy of copyright material on the Internet is an ongoing problem across all media. If you come across any illegal copies of our works, in any form, on the Internet, please provide us with the location address or website name immediately so that we can pursue a remedy.

Please contact us at legal@dynamicscompanions.com with a link to the suspected pirated material.

We appreciate your help in protecting our authors, and our ability to bring you valuable content.

Questions

You can contact us at help@dynamicscompanions.com if you are having a problem with any aspect of the book, and we will do our best to address it.

Table of Contents

DYNAMICS COMPANIONS
BARE BONES CONFIGURATION GUIDE

CONFIGURING PRODUCT INFORMATION MANAGEMENT WITHIN DYNAMICS 365 FOR OPERATIONS
MODULE 1: CONFIGURING THE PRODUCT INFORMATION MANAGEMENT CONTROLS

Introduction

Before we start creating products within the Product Information Management area of Dynamics 365, there are a couple of codes that need to configured so that everything will run smoothly. In this section we will walk through everything that you need to set up to get the basic Product Information Management features working.

Topics Covered

- Configuring Storage Dimension Groups

- Configuring Product Tracking Dimensions

- Configuring the Units Of Measure

- Review

www.dynamicscompanions.com
Dynamics Companions

- 7 -

www.blindsquirrelpublishing.com
© 2017 Blind Squirrel Publishing, LLC, All Rights Reserved

BLIND SQUIRREL
PUBLISHING

DYNAMICS COMPANIONS
BARE BONES CONFIGURATION GUIDE

CONFIGURING PRODUCT INFORMATION MANAGEMENT WITHIN DYNAMICS 365 FOR OPERATIONS
MODULE 1: CONFIGURING THE PRODUCT INFORMATION MANAGEMENT CONTROLS

Configuring Storage Dimension Groups

First we will need to set up we need to set up the **Storage Dimension Groups**. These allow us to control the level to which we track the location of the products.

Topics Covered

Opening the Storage dimension groups form

Creating a Site Storage Dimension Group

Creating a Warehouse Storage Dimension Group

Creating a Location Storage Dimension Group

Summary

Opening the Storage dimension groups form

To start off we will want to open the **Storage Dimension Groups** maintenance form which will allow us to configure all of the ways that we will be able to manage the storage of our products.

How to do it...

Step 1: Open the Storage Dimension Groups form through the menu

We can get to the **Storage dimension groups** form a couple of different ways. The first way is through the master menu.

Navigate to Product Information Management > Setup > Dimension and variant groups > Storage Dimension Groups

Step 2: Open the Storage Dimension Groups form through the menu search

Another way that we can find the **Storage dimension groups** form is through the menu search feature.

Type in **storage** into the menu search and select **Storage dimension groups**

Step 3: The Storage dimension group form

This will open up the **Storage dimension groups** maintenance form where we will be able to define the levels that our products will be stored within the system.

DYNAMICS COMPANIONS
BARE BONES CONFIGURATION GUIDE

CONFIGURING PRODUCT INFORMATION MANAGEMENT WITHIN DYNAMICS 365 FOR OPERATIONS
MODULE 1: CONFIGURING THE PRODUCT INFORMATION MANAGEMENT CONTROLS

Opening the Storage dimension groups form

How to do it...

Step 1: Open the Storage Dimension Groups form through the menu

We can get to the **Storage dimension groups** form a couple of different ways. The first way is through the master menu.

To do this, open up the navigation panel, expand out the **Modules** group, and click on **General Ledger** module to see all of the menu items that are available. Then click on the **Storage dimension groups** menu item within the **Dimension and variant** menu group.

dync
www.dynamicscompanions.com
Dynamics Companions

- 10 -

www.blindsquirrelpublishing.com
© 2017 Blind Squirrel Publishing, LLC , All Rights Reserved

BLIND SQUIRREL
PUBLISHING

DYNAMICS COMPANIONS
BARE BONES CONFIGURATION GUIDE

CONFIGURING PRODUCT INFORMATION MANAGEMENT WITHIN DYNAMICS 365 FOR OPERATIONS
MODULE 1: CONFIGURING THE PRODUCT INFORMATION MANAGEMENT CONTROLS

Opening the Storage dimension groups form

How to do it...

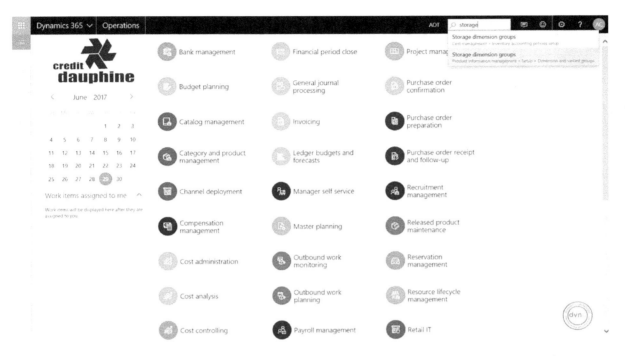

Step 2: Open the Storage Dimension Groups form through the menu search

Another way that we can find the **Storage dimension groups** form is through the menu search feature.

We can do this by clicking on the search icon in the header of the form (or by pressing **ALT+G**) and then type in **storage** into the search box. Then you will be able to select the **Storage dimension groups** maintenance form from the dropdown list.

www.dynamicscompanions.com
Dynamics Companions

- 11 -

www.blindsquirrelpublishing.com
© 2017 Blind Squirrel Publishing, LLC, All Rights Reserved

BLIND SQUIRREL
PUBLISHING

DYNAMICS COMPANIONS
BARE BONES CONFIGURATION GUIDE

CONFIGURING PRODUCT INFORMATION MANAGEMENT WITHIN DYNAMICS 365 FOR OPERATIONS
MODULE 1: CONFIGURING THE PRODUCT INFORMATION MANAGEMENT CONTROLS

Opening the Storage dimension groups form

How to do it...

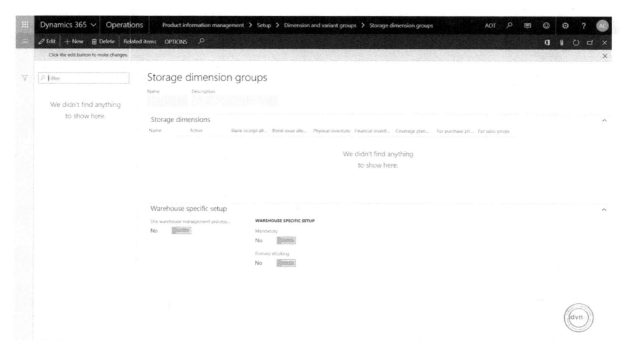

Step 3: The Storage dimension group form

This will open up the **Storage dimension groups** maintenance form where we will be able to define the levels that our products will be stored within the system.

www.dynamicscompanions.com
Dynamics Companions

- 12 -

www.blindsquirrelpublishing.com
© 2017 Blind Squirrel Publishing, LLC , All Rights Reserved

BLIND SQUIRREL
PUBLISHING

DYNAMICS COMPANIONS
BARE BONES CONFIGURATION GUIDE

CONFIGURING PRODUCT INFORMATION MANAGEMENT WITHIN DYNAMICS 365 FOR OPERATIONS
MODULE 1: CONFIGURING THE PRODUCT INFORMATION MANAGEMENT CONTROLS

Creating a Site Storage Dimension Group

The first **Storage dimension group** that we will configure is one that will allow us to mark a product to be stored and tracked at the **Site** level.

This is useful for products that don't need to be tracked at the warehouse or location level because we won't be asked to provide locations or warehouse information when we are recording the product inventory.

How to do it...

Step 1: Create a new Storage dimension group record

Now we will want to add a new **Storage dimension groups** record.

Click on the **New** button

Step 2: Give the Storage dimension group a Name

Now we will want to give our **Storage dimension group** a **Name** that we will use to reference it within the system.

Type **SITE** into the **Name** field

Step 3: Add a Description to the Storage dimension group

Next we will want to add a **Description** to the **Storage dimension group** that is a little more descriptive for the users.

Type **Site** into the **Description** field

Step 4: Save the Storage dimension group

Now we will want to save the new **Storage dimension group** record.

Click on the **Save** button

Step 5: Uncheck the Coverage Plan by Dimension for the Warehouse

For this **Storage dimension group** we will only want to plan all of our product requirements at the site level.

Uncheck the Warehouse Coverage Plan by Dimension flag

www.dynamicscompanions.com
Dynamics Companions

- 13 -

www.blindsquirrelpublishing.com
© 2017 Blind Squirrel Publishing, LLC , All Rights Reserved

BLIND SQUIRREL
PUBLISHING

DYNAMICS COMPANIONS
BARE BONES CONFIGURATION GUIDE

CONFIGURING PRODUCT INFORMATION MANAGEMENT WITHIN DYNAMICS 365 FOR OPERATIONS
MODULE 1: CONFIGURING THE PRODUCT INFORMATION MANAGEMENT CONTROLS

Creating a Site Storage Dimension Group

How to do it...

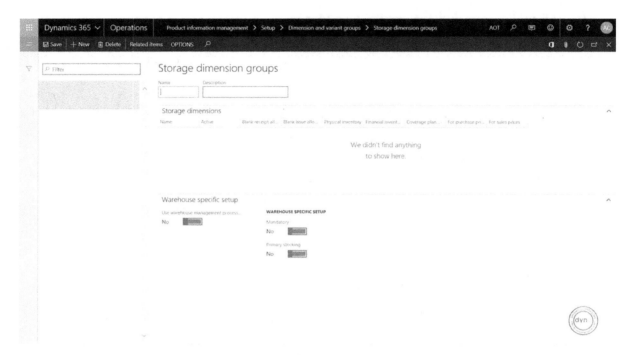

Step 1: Create a new Storage dimension group record

Now we will want to add a new **Storage dimension groups** record.

To do this, just click on the **New** button within the menu bar.

dync
www.dynamicscompanions.com
Dynamics Companions

- 14 -

www.blindsquirrelpublishing.com
© 2017 Blind Squirrel Publishing, LLC , All Rights Reserved

BLIND SQUIRREL
PUBLISHING

DYNAMICS COMPANIONS
BARE BONES CONFIGURATION GUIDE

CONFIGURING PRODUCT INFORMATION MANAGEMENT WITHIN DYNAMICS 365 FOR OPERATIONS
MODULE 1: CONFIGURING THE PRODUCT INFORMATION MANAGEMENT CONTROLS

Creating a Site Storage Dimension Group

How to do it...

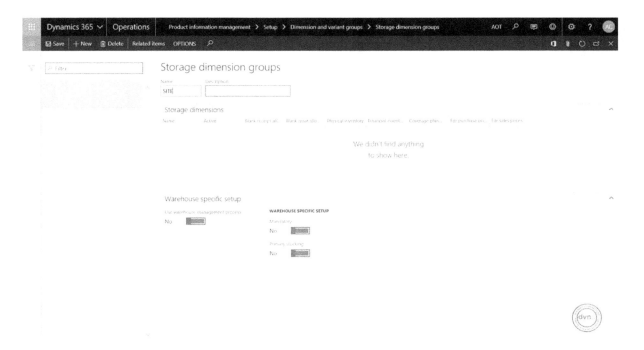

Step 2: Give the Storage dimension group a Name

Now we will want to give our **Storage dimension group** a **Name** that we will use to reference it within the system.

To do this we will just type in the code that we want to use into the **Name** field.

This **Storage dimension group** will be used to identify products that are stored at the **Site** level, so we will set the **Name** to SITE.

DYNAMICS COMPANIONS
BARE BONES CONFIGURATION GUIDE

CONFIGURING PRODUCT INFORMATION MANAGEMENT WITHIN DYNAMICS 365 FOR OPERATIONS
MODULE 1: CONFIGURING THE PRODUCT INFORMATION MANAGEMENT CONTROLS

Creating a Site Storage Dimension Group

How to do it...

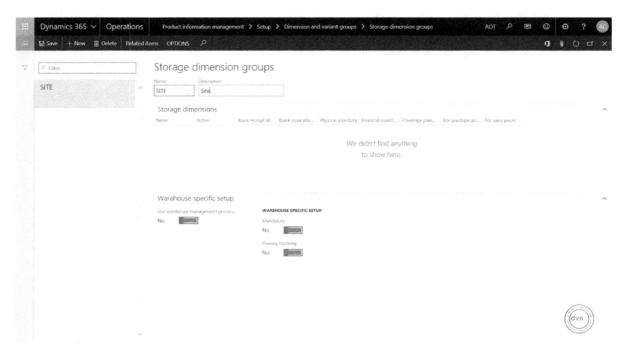

Step 3: Add a Description to the Storage dimension group

Next we will want to add a **Description** to the **Storage dimension group** that is a little more descriptive for the users.

To do this we just need to type in a better description of the **Storage dimension group** into the **Description** field.

For the SITE Storage dimension group we will set the Description to Site.

dyn c

www.dynamicscompanions.com
Dynamics Companions

- 16 -

www.blindsquirrelpublishing.com
© 2017 Blind Squirrel Publishing, LLC , All Rights Reserved

BLIND SQUIRREL
PUBLISHING

DYNAMICS COMPANIONS
BARE BONES CONFIGURATION GUIDE

CONFIGURING PRODUCT INFORMATION MANAGEMENT WITHIN DYNAMICS 365 FOR OPERATIONS
MODULE 1: CONFIGURING THE PRODUCT INFORMATION MANAGEMENT CONTROLS

Creating a Site Storage Dimension Group

How to do it...

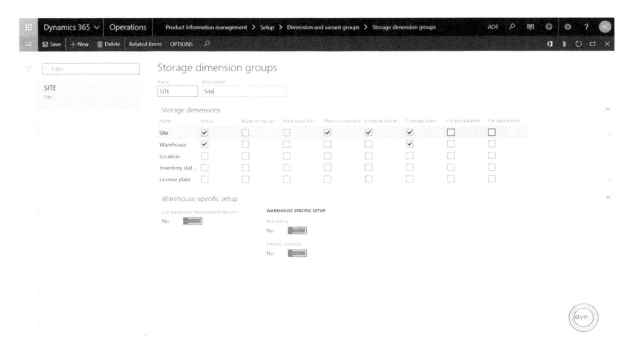

Step 4: Save the Storage dimension group

Now we will want to save the new **Storage dimension group** record.

To do this, just click on the **Save** button within the menu bar.

After you have done that you will notice that the storage dimension levels will be populated with different flags to manage how you track the storage locations.

dyn

www.dynamicscompanions.com
Dynamics Companions

- 17 -

www.blindsquirrelpublishing.com
© 2017 Blind Squirrel Publishing, LLC, All Rights Reserved

BLIND SQUIRREL
PUBLISHING

DYNAMICS COMPANIONS
BARE BONES CONFIGURATION GUIDE

CONFIGURING PRODUCT INFORMATION MANAGEMENT WITHIN DYNAMICS 365 FOR OPERATIONS
MODULE 1: CONFIGURING THE PRODUCT INFORMATION MANAGEMENT CONTROLS

Creating a Site Storage Dimension Group

How to do it...

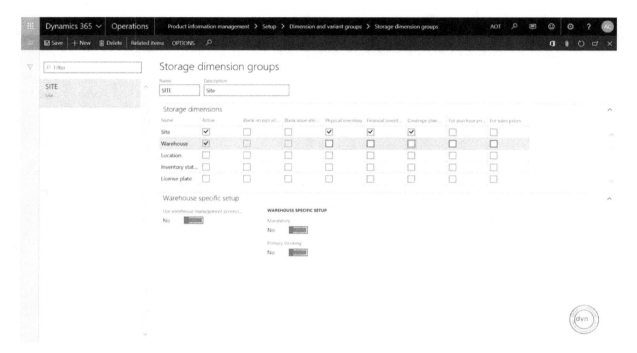

Step 5: Uncheck the Coverage Plan by Dimension for the Warehouse

For this **Storage dimension group** we will only want to plan all of our product requirements at the site level.

To do this we just need to toggle the **Coverage Plan By Dimension** flag at the **Warehouse** level.

For this storage dimension, uncheck the **Coverage Plan By Dimension** flag at the **Warehouse** level to make this only tracked at the site level.

www.dynamicscompanions.com
Dynamics Companions

- 18 -

www.blindsquirrelpublishing.com
© 2017 Blind Squirrel Publishing, LLC , All Rights Reserved

BLIND SQUIRREL
PUBLISHING

DYNAMICS COMPANIONS
BARE BONES CONFIGURATION GUIDE

CONFIGURING PRODUCT INFORMATION MANAGEMENT WITHIN DYNAMICS 365 FOR OPERATIONS
MODULE 1: CONFIGURING THE PRODUCT INFORMATION MANAGEMENT CONTROLS

Creating a Warehouse Storage Dimension Group

Next we will want to create a storage dimension that allows us to track the inventory at the warehouse level.

This is a good option for smaller warehouses where we may not have any locations marked, or where we don't track the location of the products.

How to do it...

Step 1: Create a new Storage dimension group record

Now we will want to add another **Storage dimension groups** record.

Click on the **New** button

Step 2: Give the Storage dimension group a Name

Now we will want to give our new **Storage dimension group** a **Name** to reference it within the system.

Type **WH** into the **Name** field

Step 3: Add a Description to the Storage dimension group

Now we will want to add a **Description** to the **Storage dimension group**.

Type Warehouse into the Description field

Step 4: Save the Storage dimension group

Now we will want to save the new **Storage dimension group** record.

Click on the **Save** button

Step 5: Check the Physical inventory for the Warehouse

For this **Storage dimension group** we will want to track the physical inventory at the warehouse level.

Check the Warehouse Physical inventory flag

Step 6: Confirm that the Purchase prices will be updated

This will open up a dialog box that tells us that the Purchase prices flag will automatically be checked as well.

Click on the **Yes** button

Step 7: Check the For purchase price for the Site

Since we have the **For purchase price** flag on the **Warehouse** then we will also want to do the same for the **Site.**

Check the Site For purchase price flag

www.dynamicscompanions.com
Dynamics Companions

- 19 -

www.blindsquirrelpublishing.com
© 2017 Blind Squirrel Publishing, LLC , All Rights Reserved

BLIND SQUIRREL
PUBLISHING

DYNAMICS COMPANIONS
BARE BONES CONFIGURATION GUIDE

CONFIGURING PRODUCT INFORMATION MANAGEMENT WITHIN DYNAMICS 365 FOR OPERATIONS
MODULE 1: CONFIGURING THE PRODUCT INFORMATION MANAGEMENT CONTROLS

Step 8: Confirm that update

This will open up a dialog box that tells us that the Sales prices flag will need to be checked as well.

Click on the **Yes** button.

Step 9: Check the For sales prices for the Warehouse

Since we set the purchase pricing to be controlled at the Site and Warehouse level, we will want to do the same on the sales side and allow this dimension group to be priced at the Site and Warehouse level as well.

Check the Warehouse For sales prices flag

Step 10: Check the For sales prices for the Site

Since we set the sales pricing to be controlled at the Warehouse level, then we will also want to include the Site in the pricing rules as well.

Check the Site For sales prices flag

DYNAMICS COMPANIONS
BARE BONES CONFIGURATION GUIDE

CONFIGURING PRODUCT INFORMATION MANAGEMENT WITHIN DYNAMICS 365 FOR OPERATIONS
MODULE 1: CONFIGURING THE PRODUCT INFORMATION MANAGEMENT CONTROLS

Creating a Warehouse Storage Dimension Group

How to do it...

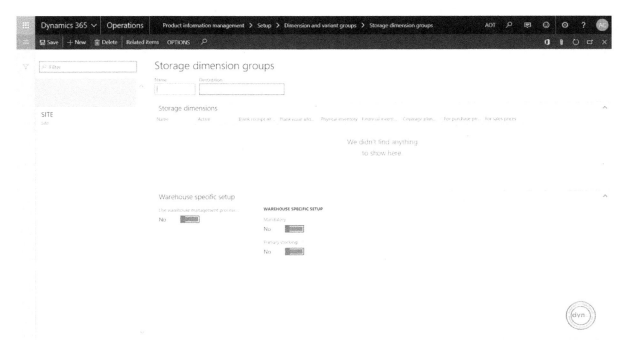

Step 1: Create a new Storage dimension group record

Now we will want to add another **Storage dimension groups** record.

To do this we just need to click on the **+ New** button

dync
www.dynamicscompanions.com
Dynamics Companions

- 21 -

www.blindsquirrelpublishing.com
© 2017 Blind Squirrel Publishing, LLC , All Rights Reserved

BLIND SQUIRREL
PUBLISHING

DYNAMICS COMPANIONS
BARE BONES CONFIGURATION GUIDE

CONFIGURING PRODUCT INFORMATION MANAGEMENT WITHIN DYNAMICS 365 FOR OPERATIONS
MODULE 1: CONFIGURING THE PRODUCT INFORMATION MANAGEMENT CONTROLS

Creating a Warehouse Storage Dimension Group

How to do it...

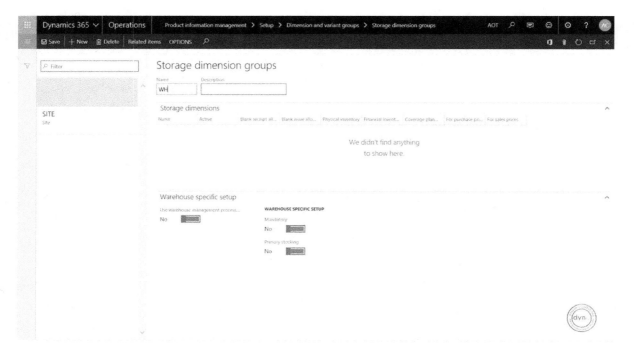

Step 2: Give the Storage dimension group a Name

Now we will want to give our new **Storage dimension group** a **Name** to reference it within the system.

To do this we will just type in the code into the **Name** field.

This **Storage dimension group** will be used to identify products that are stored at the **Warehouse** level, so we will set the **Name** to **WH**.

DYNAMICS COMPANIONS
BARE BONES CONFIGURATION GUIDE

CONFIGURING PRODUCT INFORMATION MANAGEMENT WITHIN DYNAMICS 365 FOR OPERATIONS
MODULE 1: CONFIGURING THE PRODUCT INFORMATION MANAGEMENT CONTROLS

Creating a Warehouse Storage Dimension Group

How to do it...

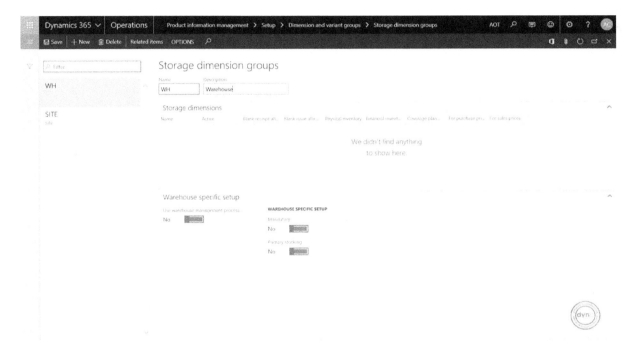

Step 3: Add a Description to the Storage dimension group

Now we will want to add a **Description** to the **Storage dimension group**.

To do this we just need to type in the description of the **Storage dimension group** into the **Description** field.

For the WH Storage dimension group we will set the Description to Warehouse.

dync

www.dynamicscompanions.com
Dynamics Companions

- 23 -

www.blindsquirrelpublishing.com
© 2017 Blind Squirrel Publishing, LLC , All Rights Reserved

BLIND SQUIRREL
PUBLISHING

DYNAMICS COMPANIONS
BARE BONES CONFIGURATION GUIDE

CONFIGURING PRODUCT INFORMATION MANAGEMENT WITHIN DYNAMICS 365 FOR OPERATIONS
MODULE 1: CONFIGURING THE PRODUCT INFORMATION MANAGEMENT CONTROLS

Creating a Warehouse Storage Dimension Group

How to do it...

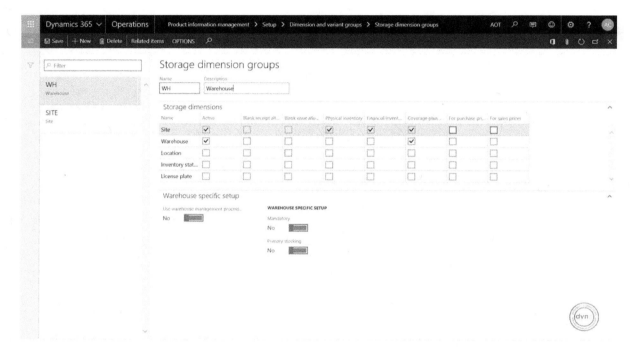

Step 4: Save the Storage dimension group

Now we will want to save the new **Storage dimension group** record.

To do this, just click on the **Save** button within the menu bar.

This will cause the storage dimension levels will be populated with different flags to manage how to track the storage locations.

www.dynamicscompanions.com
Dynamics Companions

- 24 -

www.blindsquirrelpublishing.com
© 2017 Blind Squirrel Publishing, LLC , All Rights Reserved

BLIND SQUIRREL
PUBLISHING

DYNAMICS COMPANIONS
BARE BONES CONFIGURATION GUIDE

CONFIGURING PRODUCT INFORMATION MANAGEMENT WITHIN DYNAMICS 365 FOR OPERATIONS
MODULE 1: CONFIGURING THE PRODUCT INFORMATION MANAGEMENT CONTROLS

Creating a Warehouse Storage Dimension Group

How to do it...

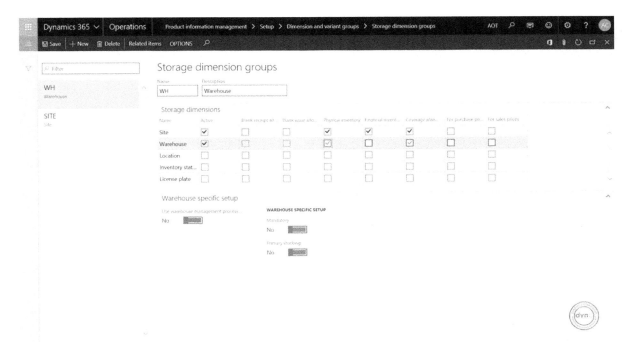

Step 5: Check the Physical inventory for the Warehouse

For this **Storage dimension group** we will want to track the physical inventory at the warehouse level.

To do this we just need to toggle the **Physical inventory** flag at the **Warehouse** level.

For this storage dimension, we will want to track the physical inventory at the warehouse level, so we will check the **Physical inventory** flag at the **Warehouse** level.

www.dynamicscompanions.com
Dynamics Companions

- 25 -

www.blindsquirrelpublishing.com
© 2017 Blind Squirrel Publishing, LLC , All Rights Reserved

BLIND SQUIRREL
PUBLISHING

DYNAMICS COMPANIONS
BARE BONES CONFIGURATION GUIDE

CONFIGURING PRODUCT INFORMATION MANAGEMENT WITHIN DYNAMICS 365 FOR OPERATIONS
MODULE 1: CONFIGURING THE PRODUCT INFORMATION MANAGEMENT CONTROLS

Creating a Warehouse Storage Dimension Group

How to do it...

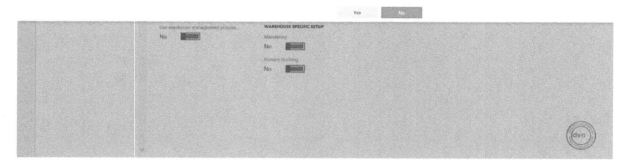

Step 6: Confirm that the Purchase prices will be updated

This will open up a dialog box that tells us that the Purchase prices flag will automatically be checked as well.

All we need to here is click on the **Yes** button to confirm the update.

www.dynamicscompanions.com
Dynamics Companions

- 26 -

www.blindsquirrelpublishing.com
© 2017 Blind Squirrel Publishing, LLC , All Rights Reserved

BLIND SQUIRREL
PUBLISHING

DYNAMICS COMPANIONS
BARE BONES CONFIGURATION GUIDE

CONFIGURING PRODUCT INFORMATION MANAGEMENT WITHIN DYNAMICS 365 FOR OPERATIONS
MODULE 1: CONFIGURING THE PRODUCT INFORMATION MANAGEMENT CONTROLS

Creating a Warehouse Storage Dimension Group

How to do it...

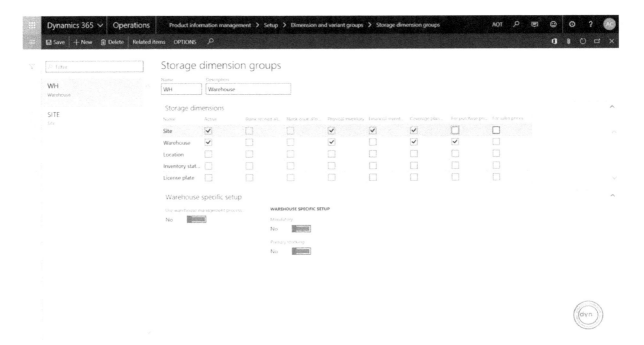

Step 6: Confirm that the Purchase prices will be updated

When we return back to the screen we will see that the **For purchase prices** flag has been set at the **Warehouse** level.

www.dynamicscompanions.com
Dynamics Companions

- 27 -

www.blindsquirrelpublishing.com
© 2017 Blind Squirrel Publishing, LLC, All Rights Reserved

BLIND SQUIRREL
PUBLISHING

DYNAMICS COMPANIONS
BARE BONES CONFIGURATION GUIDE

CONFIGURING PRODUCT INFORMATION MANAGEMENT WITHIN DYNAMICS 365 FOR OPERATIONS
MODULE 1: CONFIGURING THE PRODUCT INFORMATION MANAGEMENT CONTROLS

Creating a Warehouse Storage Dimension Group

How to do it...

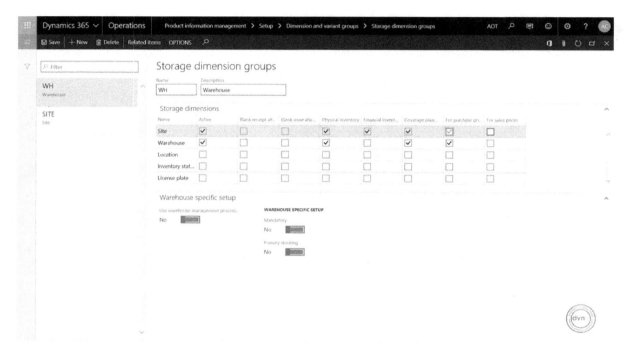

Step 7: Check the For purchase price for the Site

Since we have the **For purchase price** flag on the **Warehouse** then we will also want to do the same for the **Site.**

To do this we just need to toggle the **For purchase price** flag at the **Site** level.

For this storage dimension, we will want to track the have the ability to track purchase process at the site level, so we will check the **For purchase price** flag at the **Site** level.

www.dynamicscompanions.com
Dynamics Companions

- 28 -

www.blindsquirrelpublishing.com
© 2017 Blind Squirrel Publishing, LLC , All Rights Reserved

BLIND SQUIRREL
PUBLISHING

DYNAMICS COMPANIONS
BARE BONES CONFIGURATION GUIDE

CONFIGURING PRODUCT INFORMATION MANAGEMENT WITHIN DYNAMICS 365 FOR OPERATIONS
MODULE 1: CONFIGURING THE PRODUCT INFORMATION MANAGEMENT CONTROLS

Creating a Warehouse Storage Dimension Group

How to do it...

Step 8: Confirm that update

This will open up a dialog box that tells us that the Sales prices flag will need to be checked as well.

All we need to here is click on the **Yes** button to confirm the update.

www.dynamicscompanions.com
Dynamics Companions

- 29 -

www.blindsquirrelpublishing.com
© 2017 Blind Squirrel Publishing, LLC , All Rights Reserved

BLIND SQUIRREL
PUBLISHING

DYNAMICS COMPANIONS
BARE BONES CONFIGURATION GUIDE

CONFIGURING PRODUCT INFORMATION MANAGEMENT WITHIN DYNAMICS 365 FOR OPERATIONS
MODULE 1: CONFIGURING THE PRODUCT INFORMATION MANAGEMENT CONTROLS

Creating a Warehouse Storage Dimension Group

How to do it...

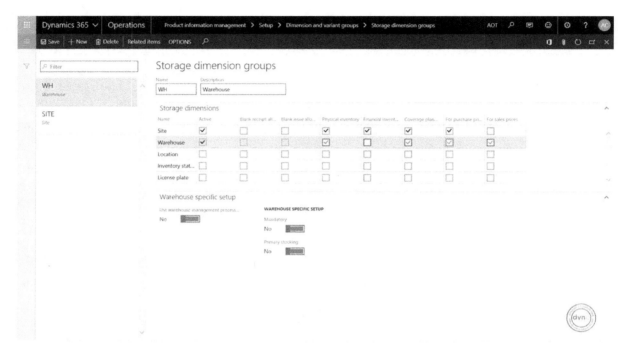

Step 9: Check the For sales prices for the Warehouse

Since we set the purchase pricing to be controlled at the Site and Warehouse level, we will want to do the same on the sales side and allow this dimension group to be priced at the Site and Warehouse level as well.

To do this, we start off and toggle the **For sales prices** flag at the **Warehouse** level.

For this storage dimension group we want the Sales priced to be controlled at the Warehouse level, so we will want to check the **Warehouse For sales prices** flag.

www.dynamicscompanions.com
Dynamics Companions

- 30 -

www.blindsquirrelpublishing.com
© 2017 Blind Squirrel Publishing, LLC, All Rights Reserved

BLIND SQUIRREL
PUBLISHING

Creating a Warehouse Storage Dimension Group

How to do it...

Step 10: Check the For sales prices for the Site

Since we set the sales pricing to be controlled at the Warehouse level, then we will also want to include the Site in the pricing rules as well.

To do this, we will also toggle the **For sales prices** flag at the **Site** level.

For this storage dimension group we want the Sales priced to be controlled at the Site level, so we will want to check the **Site For sales prices** flag.

dyn
www.dynamicscompanions.com
Dynamics Companions
- 31 -
www.blindsquirrelpublishing.com
© 2017 Blind Squirrel Publishing, LLC , All Rights Reserved
BLIND SQUIRREL
PUBLISHING

DYNAMICS COMPANIONS
BARE BONES CONFIGURATION GUIDE

CONFIGURING PRODUCT INFORMATION MANAGEMENT WITHIN DYNAMICS 365 FOR OPERATIONS
MODULE 1: CONFIGURING THE PRODUCT INFORMATION MANAGEMENT CONTROLS

Creating a Location Storage Dimension Group

Now we will want to create a storage dimension that allows us to track the inventory at the location level within our warehouses.

This is a good option for warehouses where we have designated locations that we want to store our products in and where we want to track where the products have been put so that we can easily find them.

This can apply to smaller warehouses as well where they may have racks, bins or drawers that you may be storing smaller items in.

How to do it...

Step 1: Create a new Storage dimension group record

Now we will want to add a final **Storage dimension groups** record.

Click on the **New** button

Step 2: Give the Storage dimension group a Name

Now we will want to give our new **Storage dimension group** a **Name** to reference it within the system.

Type **LOC** into the **Name** field

Step 3: Add a Description to the Storage dimension group

Now we will want to add a **Description** to the **Storage dimension group**.

Type **Location** into the **Description** field

Step 4: Save the Storage dimension group

Now we will want to save the new **Storage dimension group** record.

Click on the **Save** button

Step 5: Activate the Location tracking level

Now we will want to track the inventory at the **Location** level as well.

Check the **Location Name** flag

Step 6: Enable inventory tracking by Warehouse

Now we will want to make a few changes to the way that we track the **Physical inventory** and we will want to start off by marking it to track at the **Warehouse** level.

Check the Warehouse Physical inventory flag

Click on the **Save** button

www.dynamicscompanions.com
Dynamics Companions

- 32 -

www.blindsquirrelpublishing.com
© 2017 Blind Squirrel Publishing, LLC , All Rights Reserved

BLIND SQUIRREL
PUBLISHING

DYNAMICS COMPANIONS
BARE BONES CONFIGURATION GUIDE

CONFIGURING PRODUCT INFORMATION MANAGEMENT WITHIN DYNAMICS 365 FOR OPERATIONS
MODULE 1: CONFIGURING THE PRODUCT INFORMATION MANAGEMENT CONTROLS

Step 7: Confirm that the Purchase prices will be updated

This will open up a dialog box that tells us that the Purchase prices flag will automatically be checked as well.

Click on the **Yes** button

Step 8: Check the For purchase price for the Site

Since we have the **For purchase price** flag on the **Warehouse** then we will also want to do the same for the **Site.**

Check the Site For purchase price flag

Step 9: Confirm that update

This will open up a dialog box that tells us that the Sales prices flag will need to be checked as well.

Click on the **Yes** button.

Step 10: Check the For sales prices for the Warehouse

Since we set the purchase pricing to be controlled at the Site and Warehouse level, we will want to do the same on the sales side and allow this dimension group to be priced at the Site and Warehouse level as well.

Check the Warehouse For sales prices flag

Step 11: Check the For sales prices for the Site

Since we set the sales pricing to be controlled at the Warehouse level, then we will also want to include the Site in the pricing rules as well.

Check the Site For sales prices flag

DYNAMICS COMPANIONS
BARE BONES CONFIGURATION GUIDE

CONFIGURING PRODUCT INFORMATION MANAGEMENT WITHIN DYNAMICS 365 FOR OPERATIONS
MODULE 1: CONFIGURING THE PRODUCT INFORMATION MANAGEMENT CONTROLS

Creating a Location Storage Dimension Group

How to do it...

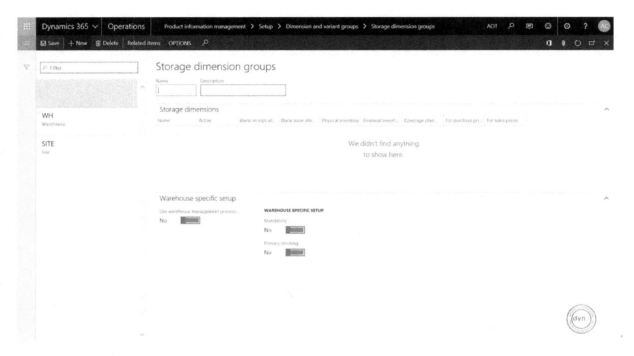

Step 1: Create a new Storage dimension group record

Now we will want to add a final **Storage dimension groups** record.

To do this we just need to click on the **+ New** button

dync
www.dynamicscompanions.com
Dynamics Companions

- 34 -

www.blindsquirrelpublishing.com
© 2017 Blind Squirrel Publishing, LLC , All Rights Reserved

BLIND SQUIRREL
PUBLISHING

DYNAMICS COMPANIONS
BARE BONES CONFIGURATION GUIDE

CONFIGURING PRODUCT INFORMATION MANAGEMENT WITHIN DYNAMICS 365 FOR OPERATIONS
MODULE 1: CONFIGURING THE PRODUCT INFORMATION MANAGEMENT CONTROLS

Creating a Location Storage Dimension Group

How to do it...

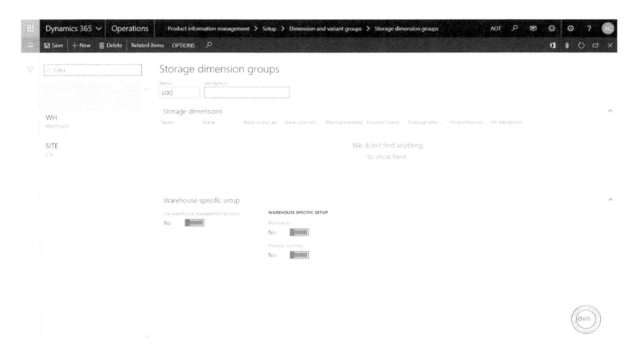

Step 2: Give the Storage dimension group a Name

Now we will want to give our new **Storage dimension group** a **Name** to reference it within the system.

To do this we will just type in the code into the **Name** field.

This **Storage dimension group** will be used to identify products that are stored at the **Warehouse Location** level, so we will set the **Name** to **LOC**.

www.dynamicscompanions.com
Dynamics Companions

- 35 -

www.blindsquirrelpublishing.com
© 2017 Blind Squirrel Publishing, LLC, All Rights Reserved

BLIND SQUIRREL
PUBLISHING

DYNAMICS COMPANIONS
BARE BONES CONFIGURATION GUIDE

CONFIGURING PRODUCT INFORMATION MANAGEMENT WITHIN DYNAMICS 365 FOR OPERATIONS
MODULE 1: CONFIGURING THE PRODUCT INFORMATION MANAGEMENT CONTROLS

Creating a Location Storage Dimension Group

How to do it...

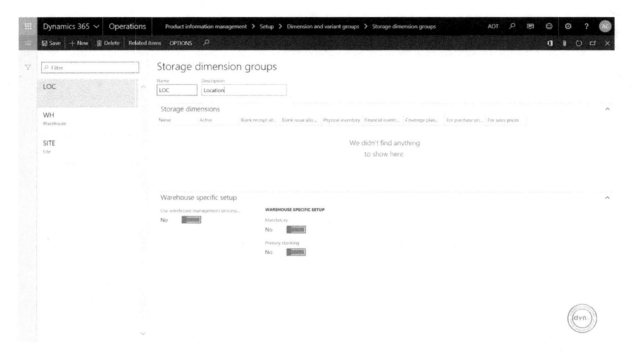

Step 3: Add a Description to the Storage dimension group

Now we will want to add a **Description** to the **Storage dimension group**.

To do this we just need to type in the description of the **Storage dimension group** into the **Description** field.

For the LOC Storage dimension group we will set the Description to Location.

www.dynamicscompanions.com
Dynamics Companions

- 36 -

www.blindsquirrelpublishing.com
© 2017 Blind Squirrel Publishing, LLC, All Rights Reserved

BLIND SQUIRREL
PUBLISHING

DYNAMICS COMPANIONS
BARE BONES CONFIGURATION GUIDE

CONFIGURING PRODUCT INFORMATION MANAGEMENT WITHIN DYNAMICS 365 FOR OPERATIONS
MODULE 1: CONFIGURING THE PRODUCT INFORMATION MANAGEMENT CONTROLS

Creating a Location Storage Dimension Group

How to do it...

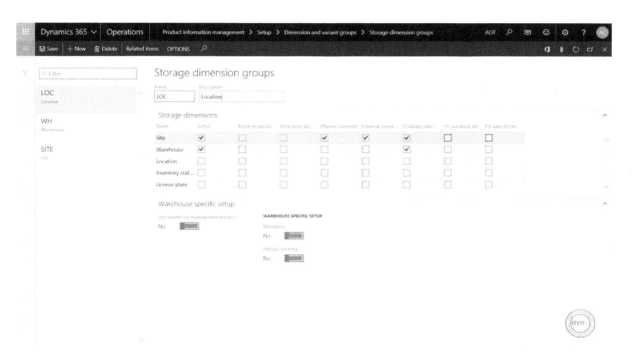

Step 4: Save the Storage dimension group

Now we will want to save the new **Storage dimension group** record.

To do this, just click on the **Save** button within the menu bar.

This will cause the storage dimension levels will be populated with different flags to manage how to track the storage locations.

www.dynamicscompanions.com
Dynamics Companions

- 37 -

www.blindsquirrelpublishing.com
© 2017 Blind Squirrel Publishing, LLC , All Rights Reserved

BLIND SQUIRREL
PUBLISHING

DYNAMICS COMPANIONS
BARE BONES CONFIGURATION GUIDE

CONFIGURING PRODUCT INFORMATION MANAGEMENT WITHIN DYNAMICS 365 FOR OPERATIONS
MODULE 1: CONFIGURING THE PRODUCT INFORMATION MANAGEMENT CONTROLS

Creating a Location Storage Dimension Group

How to do it...

Step 5: Activate the Location tracking level

Now we will want to track the inventory at the **Location** level as well.

To do this we just need to toggle the **Location** mane within the **Storage dimensions**.

For this **Storage dimension group** we will just check the **Location Name** check box within the Storage dimensions, which will enable us to track inventory at the location level.

www.dynamicscompanions.com
Dynamics Companions

- 38 -

www.blindsquirrelpublishing.com
© 2017 Blind Squirrel Publishing, LLC , All Rights Reserved

BLIND SQUIRREL
PUBLISHING

DYNAMICS COMPANIONS
BARE BONES CONFIGURATION GUIDE

CONFIGURING PRODUCT INFORMATION MANAGEMENT WITHIN DYNAMICS 365 FOR OPERATIONS
MODULE 1: CONFIGURING THE PRODUCT INFORMATION MANAGEMENT CONTROLS

Creating a Location Storage Dimension Group

How to do it...

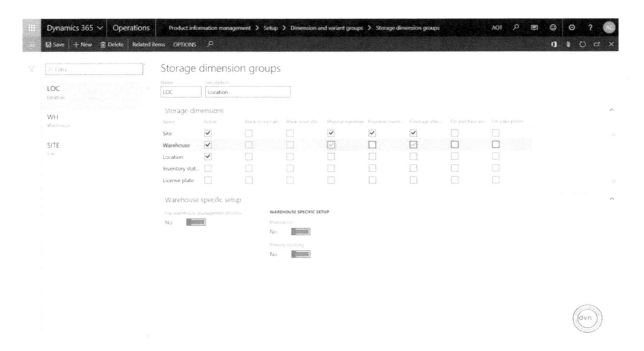

Step 6: Enable inventory tracking by Warehouse

Now we will want to make a few changes to the way that we track the **Physical inventory** and we will want to start off by marking it to track at the **Warehouse** level.

To do this we will want to toggle the **Physical inventory** flag on the **Warehouse** storage dimension.

For this example, to mark the **Storage dimension group** to track the inventory by warehouse we just check the **Physical inventory** flag at the **Warehouse** level.

www.dynamicscompanions.com
Dynamics Companions

- 39 -

www.blindsquirrelpublishing.com
© 2017 Blind Squirrel Publishing, LLC, All Rights Reserved

BLIND SQUIRREL
PUBLISHING

DYNAMICS COMPANIONS
BARE BONES CONFIGURATION GUIDE

CONFIGURING PRODUCT INFORMATION MANAGEMENT WITHIN DYNAMICS 365 FOR OPERATIONS
MODULE 1: CONFIGURING THE PRODUCT INFORMATION MANAGEMENT CONTROLS

Creating a Location Storage Dimension Group

How to do it...

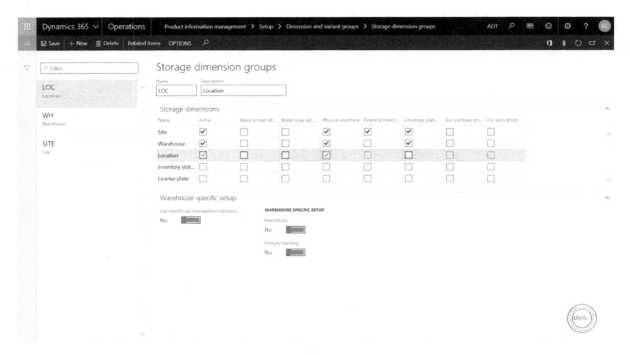

Step 6: Enable inventory tracking by Warehouse

Then check the **Physical Inventory** flags for both the **Warehouse** and the **Location**.

To do this, just click on the **Save** button within the menu bar.

www.dynamicscompanions.com
Dynamics Companions

- 40 -

www.blindsquirrelpublishing.com
© 2017 Blind Squirrel Publishing, LLC , All Rights Reserved

BLIND SQUIRREL
PUBLISHING

DYNAMICS COMPANIONS
BARE BONES CONFIGURATION GUIDE

CONFIGURING PRODUCT INFORMATION MANAGEMENT WITHIN DYNAMICS 365 FOR OPERATIONS
MODULE 1: CONFIGURING THE PRODUCT INFORMATION MANAGEMENT CONTROLS

Creating a Location Storage Dimension Group

How to do it...

Step 7: Confirm that the Purchase prices will be updated

This will open up a dialog box that tells us that the Purchase prices flag will automatically be checked as well.

All we need to here is click on the **Yes** button to confirm the update.

dyn

www.dynamicscompanions.com
Dynamics Companions

- 41 -

www.blindsquirrelpublishing.com
© 2017 Blind Squirrel Publishing, LLC , All Rights Reserved

 BLIND SQUIRREL
PUBLISHING

DYNAMICS COMPANIONS
BARE BONES CONFIGURATION GUIDE

CONFIGURING PRODUCT INFORMATION MANAGEMENT WITHIN DYNAMICS 365 FOR OPERATIONS
MODULE 1: CONFIGURING THE PRODUCT INFORMATION MANAGEMENT CONTROLS

Creating a Location Storage Dimension Group

How to do it...

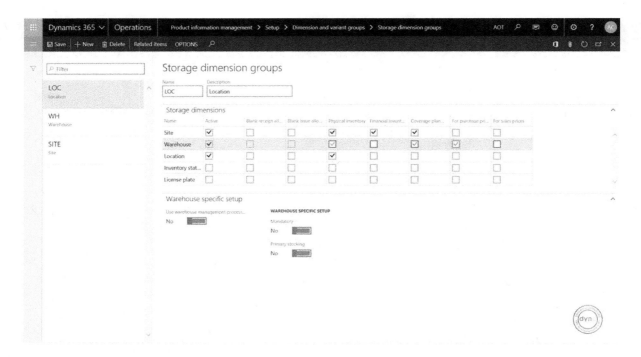

Step 7: Confirm that the Purchase prices will be updated

When we return back to the screen we will see that the **For purchase prices** flag has been set at the **Warehouse** level.

www.dynamicscompanions.com
Dynamics Companions

- 42 -

www.blindsquirrelpublishing.com
© 2017 Blind Squirrel Publishing, LLC , All Rights Reserved

BLIND SQUIRREL
PUBLISHING

DYNAMICS COMPANIONS
BARE BONES CONFIGURATION GUIDE

CONFIGURING PRODUCT INFORMATION MANAGEMENT WITHIN DYNAMICS 365 FOR OPERATIONS
MODULE 1: CONFIGURING THE PRODUCT INFORMATION MANAGEMENT CONTROLS

Creating a Location Storage Dimension Group

How to do it...

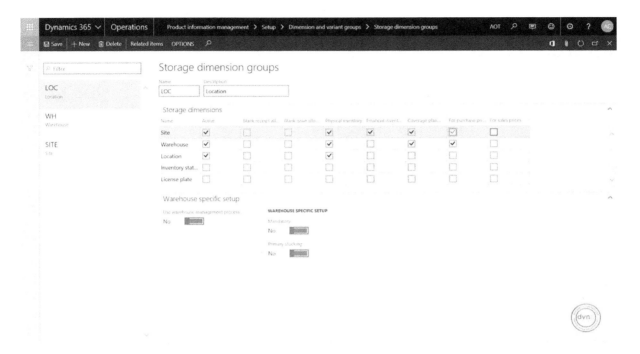

Step 8: Check the For purchase price for the Site

Since we have the **For purchase price** flag on the **Warehouse** then we will also want to do the same for the **Site.**

To do this we just need to toggle the **For purchase price** flag at the **Site** level.

For this storage dimension, we will want to track the have the ability to track purchase process at the site level, so we will check the **For purchase price** flag at the **Site** level.

dyn c
www.dynamicscompanions.com
Dynamics Companions

- 43 -

www.blindsquirrelpublishing.com
© 2017 Blind Squirrel Publishing, LLC , All Rights Reserved

BLIND SQUIRREL
PUBLISHING

DYNAMICS COMPANIONS
BARE BONES CONFIGURATION GUIDE

CONFIGURING PRODUCT INFORMATION MANAGEMENT WITHIN DYNAMICS 365 FOR OPERATIONS
MODULE 1: CONFIGURING THE PRODUCT INFORMATION MANAGEMENT CONTROLS

Creating a Location Storage Dimension Group

How to do it...

Step 9: Confirm that update

This will open up a dialog box that tells us that the Sales prices flag will need to be checked as well.

All we need to here is click on the **Yes** button to confirm the update.

www.dynamicscompanions.com
Dynamics Companions

- 44 -

www.blindsquirrelpublishing.com
© 2017 Blind Squirrel Publishing, LLC , All Rights Reserved

BLIND SQUIRREL
PUBLISHING

DYNAMICS COMPANIONS
BARE BONES CONFIGURATION GUIDE

CONFIGURING PRODUCT INFORMATION MANAGEMENT WITHIN DYNAMICS 365 FOR OPERATIONS
MODULE 1: CONFIGURING THE PRODUCT INFORMATION MANAGEMENT CONTROLS

Creating a Location Storage Dimension Group

How to do it...

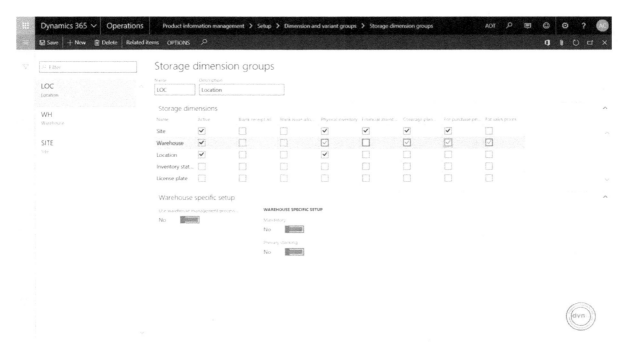

Step 10: Check the For sales prices for the Warehouse

Since we set the purchase pricing to be controlled at the Site and Warehouse level, we will want to do the same on the sales side and allow this dimension group to be priced at the Site and Warehouse level as well.

To do this we start of and toggle the **For sales prices** flag at the **Warehouse** level.

For this storage dimension group we want the Sales priced to be controlled at the Warehouse level, so we will want to check the **Warehouse For sales prices** flag.

www.dynamicscompanions.com
Dynamics Companions

- 45 -

www.blindsquirrelpublishing.com
© 2017 Blind Squirrel Publishing, LLC , All Rights Reserved

BLIND SQUIRREL
PUBLISHING

DYNAMICS COMPANIONS
BARE BONES CONFIGURATION GUIDE

CONFIGURING PRODUCT INFORMATION MANAGEMENT WITHIN DYNAMICS 365 FOR OPERATIONS
MODULE 1: CONFIGURING THE PRODUCT INFORMATION MANAGEMENT CONTROLS

Creating a Location Storage Dimension Group

How to do it...

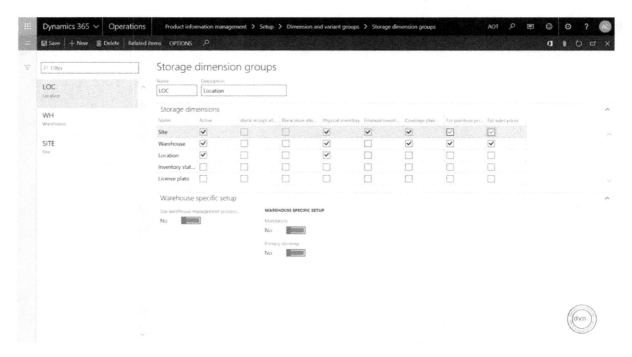

Step 11: Check the For sales prices for the Site

Since we set the sales pricing to be controlled at the Warehouse level, then we will also want to include the Site in the pricing rules as well.

Note: We don't want to check the prices for the **Location** level because that would make us track different costs for each warehouse location.

When you have done that, click on the **Close** button to exit from the form.

To do this we start of and toggle the **For sales prices** flag at the **Site** level.

For this storage dimension group we want the Sales priced to be controlled at the Site level, so we will want to check the **Site For sales prices** flag.

www.dynamicscompanions.com
Dynamics Companions

- 46 -

www.blindsquirrelpublishing.com
© 2017 Blind Squirrel Publishing, LLC , All Rights Reserved

BLIND SQUIRREL
PUBLISHING

DYNAMICS COMPANIONS
BARE BONES CONFIGURATION GUIDE

CONFIGURING PRODUCT INFORMATION MANAGEMENT WITHIN DYNAMICS 365 FOR OPERATIONS
MODULE 1: CONFIGURING THE PRODUCT INFORMATION MANAGEMENT CONTROLS

Summary

Now we have a set of **Storage dimension groups** that we can use to track how we store our products within our inventory.

www.dynamicscompanions.com
Dynamics Companions

- 47 -

www.blindsquirrelpublishing.com
© 2017 Blind Squirrel Publishing, LLC, All Rights Reserved

BLIND SQUIRREL
PUBLISHING

DYNAMICS COMPANIONS
BARE BONES CONFIGURATION GUIDE

CONFIGURING PRODUCT INFORMATION MANAGEMENT WITHIN DYNAMICS 365 FOR OPERATIONS
MODULE 1: CONFIGURING THE PRODUCT INFORMATION MANAGEMENT CONTROLS

Configuring Product Tracking Dimensions

Next we need to set up the **Product Tracking Dimensions** which are used to identify if products are going to be Batch and/or Serial Number controlled.

Topics Covered

Opening the Tracking dimension groups form

Creating a Non-Tracking Tracking Dimension Group

Creating a Batch Number Tracking Dimension Group

Creating a Serial Number Tracking Dimension Group

Creating a Batch and Serial Number Tracking Dimension Group

Summary

www.dynamicscompanions.com
Dynamics Companions

- 48 -

www.blindsquirrelpublishing.com
© 2017 Blind Squirrel Publishing, LLC , All Rights Reserved

BLIND SQUIRREL
PUBLISHING

DYNAMICS COMPANIONS
BARE BONES CONFIGURATION GUIDE

CONFIGURING PRODUCT INFORMATION MANAGEMENT WITHIN DYNAMICS 365 FOR OPERATIONS
MODULE 1: CONFIGURING THE PRODUCT INFORMATION MANAGEMENT CONTROLS

Opening the Tracking dimension groups form

To start off we will want to open the **Tracking Dimension Groups** maintenance form which will allow us to configure all of the ways that we will be able to track and identify our products.

How to do it...

Step 1: Open the Tracking Dimension Groups form through the menu

We can get to the **Tracking dimension groups** form a couple of different ways. The first way is through the master menu.

Navigate to Product Information Management > Setup > Dimension and variant groups > Storage Dimension Groups

Step 2: Open the Tracking Dimension Groups form through the menu search

Another way that we can find the **Tracking dimension groups** form is through the menu search feature.

Type in **tracking** into the menu search and select **Tracking dimension groups**

The Tracking dimension group form

DYNAMICS COMPANIONS
BARE BONES CONFIGURATION GUIDE

CONFIGURING PRODUCT INFORMATION MANAGEMENT WITHIN DYNAMICS 365 FOR OPERATIONS
MODULE 1: CONFIGURING THE PRODUCT INFORMATION MANAGEMENT CONTROLS

Opening the Tracking dimension groups form

How to do it...

Step 1: Open the Tracking Dimension Groups form through the menu

We can get to the **Tracking dimension groups** form a couple of different ways. The first way is through the master menu.

To do this, click on the **Tracking Dimension Groups** menu item within the **Dimension Groups** folder of the **Setup** group within the **Product Information Management** area page.

dyn

www.dynamicscompanions.com
Dynamics Companions

- 50 -

www.blindsquirrelpublishing.com
© 2017 Blind Squirrel Publishing, LLC , All Rights Reserved

BLIND SQUIRREL
PUBLISHING

DYNAMICS COMPANIONS
BARE BONES CONFIGURATION GUIDE

CONFIGURING PRODUCT INFORMATION MANAGEMENT WITHIN DYNAMICS 365 FOR OPERATIONS
MODULE 1: CONFIGURING THE PRODUCT INFORMATION MANAGEMENT CONTROLS

Opening the Tracking dimension groups form

How to do it...

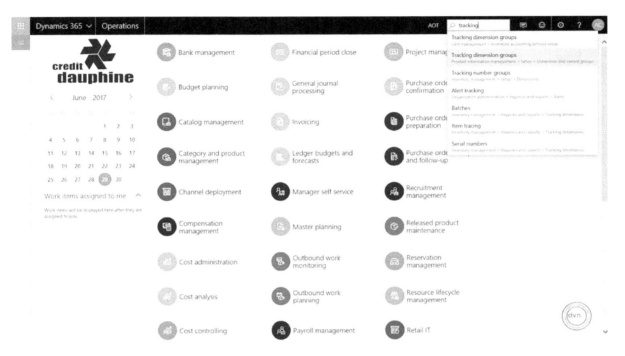

Step 2: Open the Tracking Dimension Groups form through the menu search

Another way that we can find the **Tracking dimension groups** form is through the menu search feature.

We can do this by clicking on the search icon in the header of the form (or by pressing **ALT+G)** and then type in **tracking** into the search box. Then you will be able to select the **Tracking dimension groups** maintenance form from the dropdown list.

dyn c

www.dynamicscompanions.com
Dynamics Companions

- 51 -

www.blindsquirrelpublishing.com
© 2017 Blind Squirrel Publishing, LLC, All Rights Reserved

BLIND SQUIRREL
PUBLISHING

DYNAMICS COMPANIONS
BARE BONES CONFIGURATION GUIDE

CONFIGURING PRODUCT INFORMATION MANAGEMENT WITHIN DYNAMICS 365 FOR OPERATIONS
MODULE 1: CONFIGURING THE PRODUCT INFORMATION MANAGEMENT CONTROLS

Opening the Tracking dimension groups form

How to do it...

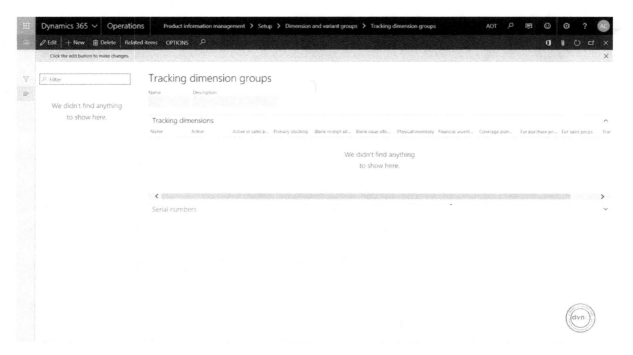

Step 2: Open the Tracking Dimension Groups form through the menu search

This will open up the **Tracking dimension groups** maintenance form where we will be able to define the levels that our products will be stored within the system.

dync
www.dynamicscompanions.com
Dynamics Companions

- 52 -

www.blindsquirrelpublishing.com
© 2017 Blind Squirrel Publishing, LLC , All Rights Reserved

BLIND SQUIRREL
PUBLISHING

DYNAMICS COMPANIONS
BARE BONES CONFIGURATION GUIDE

CONFIGURING PRODUCT INFORMATION MANAGEMENT WITHIN DYNAMICS 365 FOR OPERATIONS
MODULE 1: CONFIGURING THE PRODUCT INFORMATION MANAGEMENT CONTROLS

Creating a Non-Tracking Tracking Dimension Group

The first **Tracking dimension group** that we will configure is one that will allow us to mark a product as not tracked in any way.

This is a good option for products that you don't need to record batch or serial numbers against, and that you won't need to perform traces against from component products. Also this is a great tracking option for products that you just expense or that are completely interchangeable.

How to do it...

Step 1: Create a new Tracking dimension group

Now we will want to create a new **Tracking dimension group** record.

Click the **New** button

Step 2: Give the Tracking dimension group a Name

Now we will want to give our **Tracking dimension group** a code that we will be able to use as a reference.

Type in **NONE** into the **Name** field

Step 3: Add a Description to the Tracking dimension group

Next we will want to add a **Description** to the **Tracking dimension group** that is a little more descriptive for the users.

Set the Description to None

Step 4: Save the Tracking dimension group

Now we will want to save the new **Tracking dimension group** record.

Click the **Save** button

www.dynamicscompanions.com
Dynamics Companions

- 53 -

www.blindsquirrelpublishing.com
© 2017 Blind Squirrel Publishing, LLC , All Rights Reserved

BLIND SQUIRREL
PUBLISHING

DYNAMICS COMPANIONS
BARE BONES CONFIGURATION GUIDE

CONFIGURING PRODUCT INFORMATION MANAGEMENT WITHIN DYNAMICS 365 FOR OPERATIONS
MODULE 1: CONFIGURING THE PRODUCT INFORMATION MANAGEMENT CONTROLS

Creating a Non-Tracking Tracking Dimension Group

How to do it...

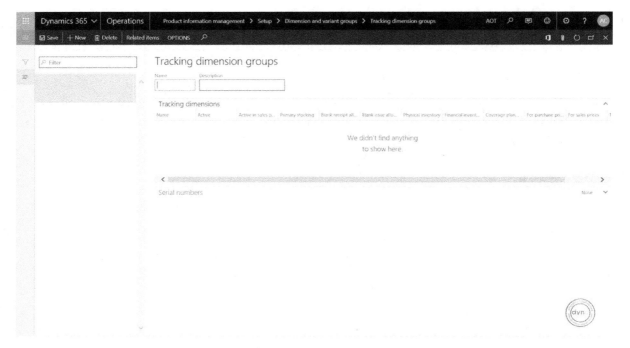

Step 1: Create a new Tracking dimension group

Now we will want to create a new **Tracking dimension group** record.

To do this, all we need to do is click on the **New** button in the menu bar and this will create a new record for us.

www.dynamicscompanions.com
Dynamics Companions

- 54 -

www.blindsquirrelpublishing.com
© 2017 Blind Squirrel Publishing, LLC , All Rights Reserved

BLIND SQUIRREL
PUBLISHING

DYNAMICS COMPANIONS
BARE BONES CONFIGURATION GUIDE

CONFIGURING PRODUCT INFORMATION MANAGEMENT WITHIN DYNAMICS 365 FOR OPERATIONS
MODULE 1: CONFIGURING THE PRODUCT INFORMATION MANAGEMENT CONTROLS

Creating a Non-Tracking Tracking Dimension Group

How to do it...

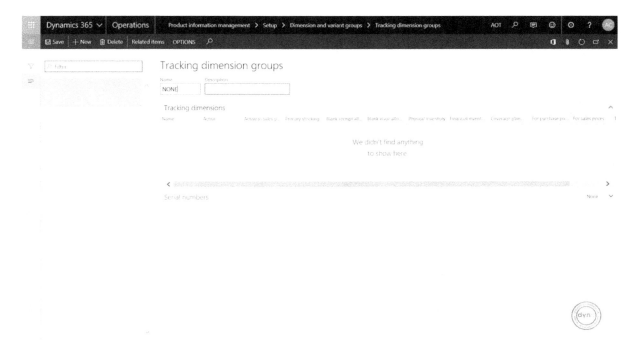

Step 2: Give the Tracking dimension group a Name

Now we will want to give our **Tracking dimension group** a code that we will be able to use as a reference.

To do this we just type in the code that we want to assign to the **Tracking dimension group** into the **Name** field.

For this **Tracking dimension group**, since we are using this to have no tracking performed then we will set the **Name** to **NONE.**

dyn

www.dynamicscompanions.com
Dynamics Companions

- 55 -

www.blindsquirrelpublishing.com
© 2017 Blind Squirrel Publishing, LLC, All Rights Reserved

BLIND SQUIRREL
PUBLISHING

DYNAMICS COMPANIONS
BARE BONES CONFIGURATION GUIDE

CONFIGURING PRODUCT INFORMATION MANAGEMENT WITHIN DYNAMICS 365 FOR OPERATIONS
MODULE 1: CONFIGURING THE PRODUCT INFORMATION MANAGEMENT CONTROLS

Creating a Non-Tracking Tracking Dimension Group

How to do it...

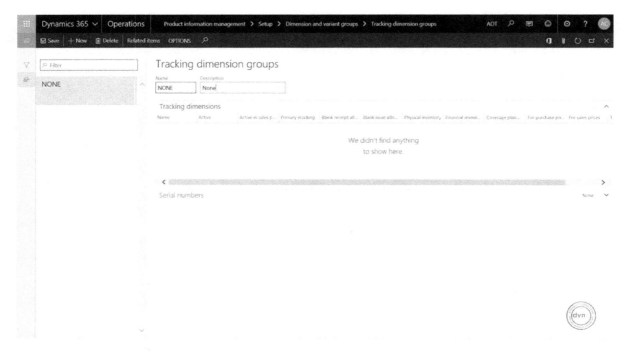

Step 3: Add a Description to the Tracking dimension group

Next we will want to add a **Description** to the **Tracking dimension group** that is a little more descriptive for the users.

To do this we just need to type in the description of the **Tracking dimension group** into the **Description** field.

For this **Tracking dimension group** we will set the **Description** to **None** to match the Name.

dync
www.dynamicscompanions.com
Dynamics Companions

- 56 -

www.blindsquirrelpublishing.com
© 2017 Blind Squirrel Publishing, LLC , All Rights Reserved

BLIND SQUIRREL
PUBLISHING

DYNAMICS COMPANIONS
BARE BONES CONFIGURATION GUIDE

CONFIGURING PRODUCT INFORMATION MANAGEMENT WITHIN DYNAMICS 365 FOR OPERATIONS
MODULE 1: CONFIGURING THE PRODUCT INFORMATION MANAGEMENT CONTROLS

Creating a Non-Tracking Tracking Dimension Group

How to do it...

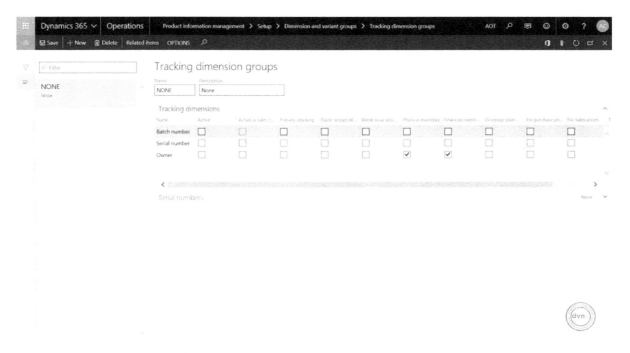

Step 4: Save the Tracking dimension group

Now we will want to save the new **Tracking dimension group** record.

To do this, we just need to click on the **Save** button in the menu bar.

After you have done that you will notice that the tracking dimension levels will be populated with different flags to manage how you track the tracking dimensions.

Because we are not tracking any dimensions with this **Tracking dimension group** then we are done with this record and can move on.

dyn

www.dynamicscompanions.com
Dynamics Companions

- 57 -

www.blindsquirrelpublishing.com
© 2017 Blind Squirrel Publishing, LLC , All Rights Reserved

BLIND SQUIRREL
PUBLISHING

DYNAMICS COMPANIONS
BARE BONES CONFIGURATION GUIDE

CONFIGURING PRODUCT INFORMATION MANAGEMENT WITHIN DYNAMICS 365 FOR OPERATIONS
MODULE 1: CONFIGURING THE PRODUCT INFORMATION MANAGEMENT CONTROLS

Creating a Batch Number Tracking Dimension Group

Another **Tracking dimension group** that we will configure is one that will allow us to mark a product to be tracked by **Batch** number.

We will use this type of **Tracking dimension group** to track both Batched and Lotted products within the system, which could be bulk products that we receive in from other vendors, or products that we create that may need to be tracked by production run.

These products are usually products that we want to keep tabs on, and may need to perform traces to see where batches or lots were received from, or used within the system.

How to do it...

Step 1: Create a new Tracking dimension group

Now we will want to create another **Tracking dimension group** record.

Click on the **New** button

Step 2: Give the Tracking dimension group a Name

Now we will want to give our **Tracking dimension group** a code that we will be able to use as a reference.

Set the **Name** to **BATCH**

Step 3: Add a Description to the Tracking dimension group

Next we will want to add a **Description** to the **Tracking dimension group** that is a little more descriptive for the users.

Set the Description to Batch Number Tracking

Step 4: Save the Tracking dimension group

Now we will want to save the new **Tracking dimension group** record.

Click on the **Save** button

Step 5: Make Batch tracking active

Now we will want to activate **Batch number** tracking on our **Tracking dimension group**.

Check the Batch number Active flag

Step 6: Mark Physical Inventory to be tracked by Batch

Before we are finish we will need to make one final change and that is to mark the inventory as being tracked at the batch number.

Check the Batch number Physical Inventory flag

dync
www.dynamicscompanions.com
Dynamics Companions

- 58 -

www.blindsquirrelpublishing.com
© 2017 Blind Squirrel Publishing, LLC , All Rights Reserved

BLIND SQUIRREL
PUBLISHING

DYNAMICS COMPANIONS
BARE BONES CONFIGURATION GUIDE

CONFIGURING PRODUCT INFORMATION MANAGEMENT WITHIN DYNAMICS 365 FOR OPERATIONS
MODULE 1: CONFIGURING THE PRODUCT INFORMATION MANAGEMENT CONTROLS

Creating a Batch Number Tracking Dimension Group

How to do it...

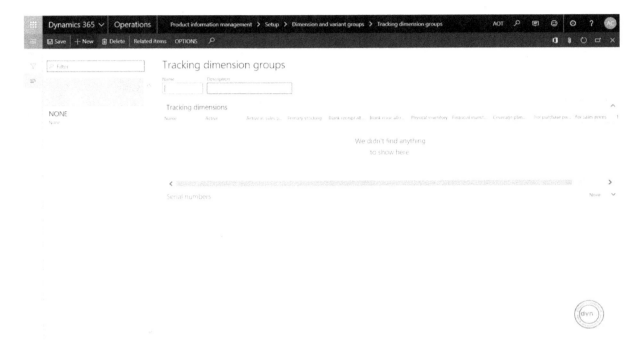

Step 1: Create a new Tracking dimension group

Now we will want to create another **Tracking dimension group** record.

To do this, all we need to do is click on the **New** button in the menu bar and this will create a new record for us.

www.dynamicscompanions.com
Dynamics Companions

- 59 -

www.blindsquirrelpublishing.com
© 2017 Blind Squirrel Publishing, LLC, All Rights Reserved

BLIND SQUIRREL
PUBLISHING

DYNAMICS COMPANIONS
BARE BONES CONFIGURATION GUIDE

CONFIGURING PRODUCT INFORMATION MANAGEMENT WITHIN DYNAMICS 365 FOR OPERATIONS
MODULE 1: CONFIGURING THE PRODUCT INFORMATION MANAGEMENT CONTROLS

Creating a Batch Number Tracking Dimension Group

How to do it...

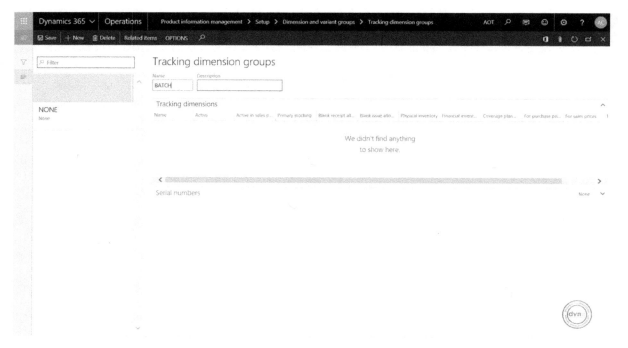

Step 2: Give the Tracking dimension group a Name

Now we will want to give our **Tracking dimension group** a code that we will be able to use as a reference.

To do this we just type in the code that we want to assign to the **Tracking dimension group** into the **Name** field.

For this **Tracking dimension group,** since we will be using this to identify products that are tracked by their batch or lot number we will set the **Name** to **BATCH**.

dync
www.dynamicscompanions.com
Dynamics Companions

- 60 -

www.blindsquirrelpublishing.com
© 2017 Blind Squirrel Publishing, LLC , All Rights Reserved

BLIND SQUIRREL
PUBLISHING

DYNAMICS COMPANIONS
BARE BONES CONFIGURATION GUIDE

CONFIGURING PRODUCT INFORMATION MANAGEMENT WITHIN DYNAMICS 365 FOR OPERATIONS
MODULE 1: CONFIGURING THE PRODUCT INFORMATION MANAGEMENT CONTROLS

Creating a Batch Number Tracking Dimension Group

How to do it...

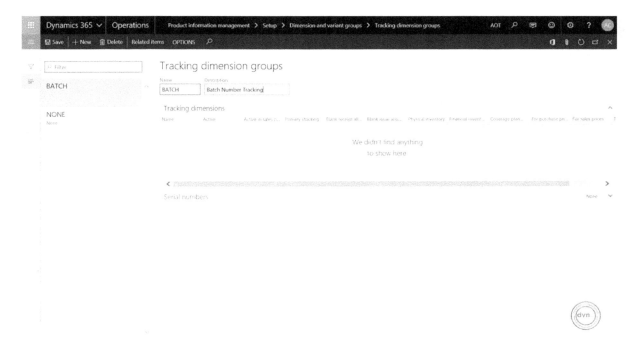

Step 3: Add a Description to the Tracking dimension group

Next we will want to add a **Description** to the **Tracking dimension group** that is a little more descriptive for the users.

To do this we just need to type in the description of the **Tracking dimension group** into the **Description** field.

For this Tracking dimension group we will set the Description to Batch Number Tracking to match the Name.

DYNAMICS COMPANIONS
BARE BONES CONFIGURATION GUIDE

CONFIGURING PRODUCT INFORMATION MANAGEMENT WITHIN DYNAMICS 365 FOR OPERATIONS
MODULE 1: CONFIGURING THE PRODUCT INFORMATION MANAGEMENT CONTROLS

Creating a Batch Number Tracking Dimension Group

How to do it...

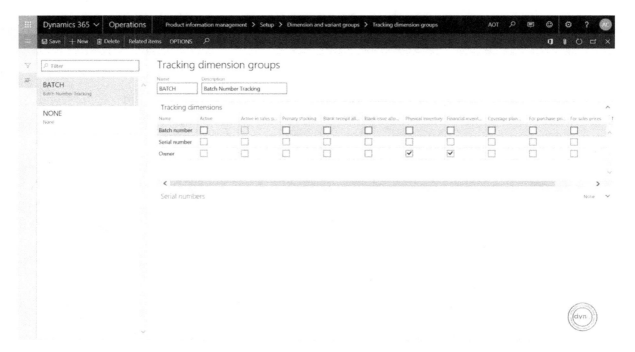

Step 4: Save the Tracking dimension group

Now we will want to save the new **Tracking dimension group** record.

To do this, we just need to click on the **Save** button in the menu bar.

After you have done that you will notice that the tracking dimension levels will be populated with different flags to manage how you track the tracking dimensions.

dyn c
www.dynamicscompanions.com
Dynamics Companions

- 62 -

www.blindsquirrelpublishing.com
© 2017 Blind Squirrel Publishing, LLC , All Rights Reserved

BLIND SQUIRREL
PUBLISHING

DYNAMICS COMPANIONS
BARE BONES CONFIGURATION GUIDE

CONFIGURING PRODUCT INFORMATION MANAGEMENT WITHIN DYNAMICS 365 FOR OPERATIONS
MODULE 1: CONFIGURING THE PRODUCT INFORMATION MANAGEMENT CONTROLS

Creating a Batch Number Tracking Dimension Group

How to do it...

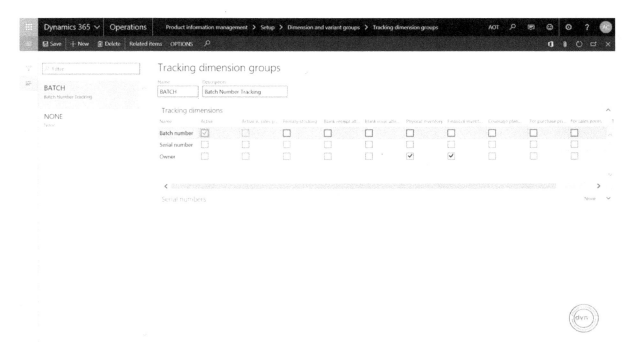

Step 5: Make Batch tracking active

Now we will want to activate **Batch number** tracking on our **Tracking dimension group**.

To do this we just need to toggle the **Active** flag on the **Batch number** tracking dimension.

For this **Tracking dimension group**, we want just the batch number tracking to be enabled, so we will want to check the **Active** flag within the **Batch number** tracking dimension line.

dyn

www.dynamicscompanions.com
Dynamics Companions

- 63 -

www.blindsquirrelpublishing.com
© 2017 Blind Squirrel Publishing, LLC, All Rights Reserved

BLIND SQUIRREL
PUBLISHING

DYNAMICS COMPANIONS
BARE BONES CONFIGURATION GUIDE

CONFIGURING PRODUCT INFORMATION MANAGEMENT WITHIN DYNAMICS 365 FOR OPERATIONS
MODULE 1: CONFIGURING THE PRODUCT INFORMATION MANAGEMENT CONTROLS

Creating a Batch Number Tracking Dimension Group

How to do it...

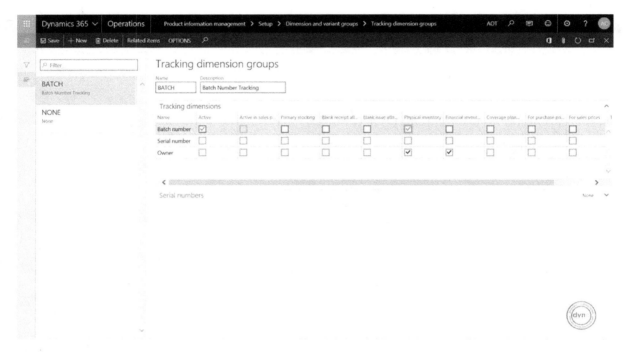

Step 6: Mark Physical Inventory to be tracked by Batch

Before we are finish we will need to make one final change and that is to mark the inventory as being tracked at the batch number.

To do this we will just want to toggle the **Physical Inventory** flag at the **Batch Number** tracking dimension.

For this **Tracking dimension group**, we want the inventory to be tracked at the batch number level, so we will want to check the **Physical inventory** flag within the **Batch number** tracking dimension line.

dync
www.dynamicscompanions.com
Dynamics Companions

- 64 -

www.blindsquirrelpublishing.com
© 2017 Blind Squirrel Publishing, LLC , All Rights Reserved

BLIND SQUIRREL
PUBLISHING

DYNAMICS COMPANIONS
BARE BONES CONFIGURATION GUIDE

CONFIGURING PRODUCT INFORMATION MANAGEMENT WITHIN DYNAMICS 365 FOR OPERATIONS
MODULE 1: CONFIGURING THE PRODUCT INFORMATION MANAGEMENT CONTROLS

Creating a Serial Number Tracking Dimension Group

Another **Tracking dimension group** that we will configure is one that will allow us to mark a product to be tracked by **Serial** number.

We will use this type of **Tracking dimension group** to track products within the system that have been identified with unique serial numbers, which could be equipment, or individually packaged products.

These products are usually products that we want to keep even tighter tabs on within the system.

How to do it...

Step 1: Create a new Tracking dimension group

Now we will want to create another **Tracking dimension group** record.

Click on the **New** button

Step 2: Give the Tracking dimension group a Name

Now we will want to give our **Tracking dimension group** a code that we will be able to use as a reference.

Set the **Name** to SERIAL

Step 3: Add a Description to the Tracking dimension group

Next we will want to add a **Description** to the **Tracking dimension group** that is a little more descriptive for the users.

Set the Description to Serial Number Tracking

Step 4: Save the Tracking dimension group

Now we will want to save the new **Tracking dimension group** record.

Click on the **Save** button

Step 5: Make Serial tracking active

Now we will want to activate **Serial number** tracking on our **Tracking dimension group**.

Check the Serial number Active flag

Step 6: Mark Physical Inventory to be tracked by Serial number

Before we are finish we will need to make one final change and that is to mark the inventory as being tracked at the serial number.

Check the Serial number Physical Inventory flag

dync

www.dynamicscompanions.com
Dynamics Companions

- 65 -

www.blindsquirrelpublishing.com
© 2017 Blind Squirrel Publishing, LLC , All Rights Reserved

 BLIND SQUIRREL
PUBLISHING

DYNAMICS COMPANIONS
BARE BONES CONFIGURATION GUIDE

CONFIGURING PRODUCT INFORMATION MANAGEMENT WITHIN DYNAMICS 365 FOR OPERATIONS
MODULE 1: CONFIGURING THE PRODUCT INFORMATION MANAGEMENT CONTROLS

Creating a Serial Number Tracking Dimension Group

How to do it...

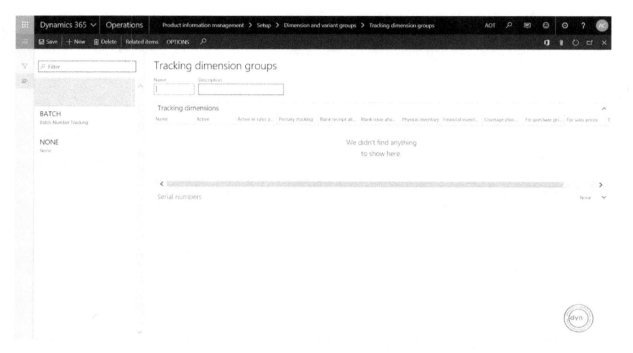

Step 1: Create a new Tracking dimension group

Now we will want to create another **Tracking dimension group** record.

To do this, all we need to do is click on the **New** button in the menu bar and this will create a new record for us.

dyn c
www.dynamicscompanions.com
Dynamics Companions

- 66 -

www.blindsquirrelpublishing.com
© 2017 Blind Squirrel Publishing, LLC , All Rights Reserved

BLIND SQUIRREL
PUBLISHING

DYNAMICS COMPANIONS
BARE BONES CONFIGURATION GUIDE

CONFIGURING PRODUCT INFORMATION MANAGEMENT WITHIN DYNAMICS 365 FOR OPERATIONS
MODULE 1: CONFIGURING THE PRODUCT INFORMATION MANAGEMENT CONTROLS

Creating a Serial Number Tracking Dimension Group

How to do it...

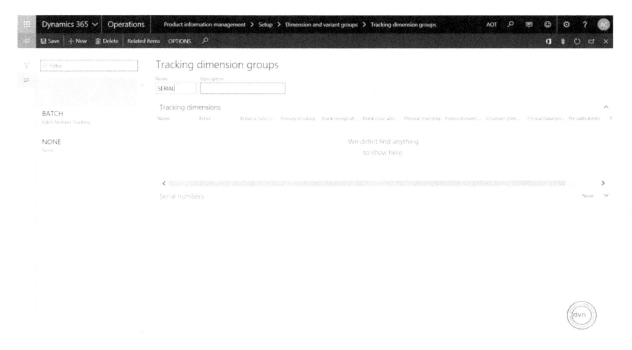

Step 2: Give the Tracking dimension group a Name

Now we will want to give our **Tracking dimension group** a code that we will be able to use as a reference.

To do this we just type in the code that we want to assign to the **Tracking dimension group** into the **Name** field.

For this **Tracking dimension group,** since we will be using this to identify products that are tracked by their serial number we will set the **Name** to **SERIAL**.

dyn
www.dynamicscompanions.com
Dynamics Companions

- 67 -

www.blindsquirrelpublishing.com
© 2017 Blind Squirrel Publishing, LLC, All Rights Reserved

BLIND SQUIRREL
PUBLISHING

DYNAMICS COMPANIONS
BARE BONES CONFIGURATION GUIDE

CONFIGURING PRODUCT INFORMATION MANAGEMENT WITHIN DYNAMICS 365 FOR OPERATIONS
MODULE 1: CONFIGURING THE PRODUCT INFORMATION MANAGEMENT CONTROLS

Creating a Serial Number Tracking Dimension Group

How to do it...

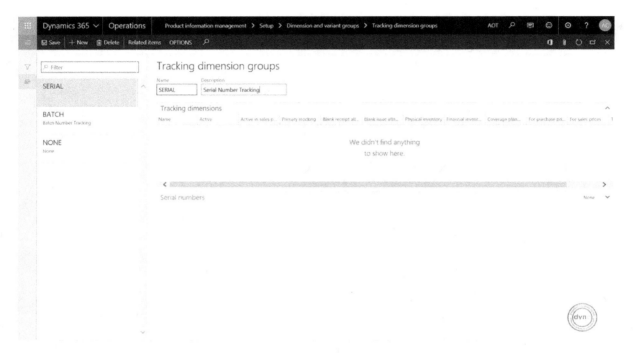

Step 3: Add a Description to the Tracking dimension group

Next we will want to add a **Description** to the **Tracking dimension group** that is a little more descriptive for the users.

To do this we just need to type in the description of the **Tracking dimension group** into the **Description** field.

For this Tracking dimension group we will set the Description to Serial Number Tracking to match the Name.

dync
www.dynamicscompanions.com
Dynamics Companions

- 68 -

www.blindsquirrelpublishing.com
© 2017 Blind Squirrel Publishing, LLC , All Rights Reserved

BLIND SQUIRREL
PUBLISHING

DYNAMICS COMPANIONS
BARE BONES CONFIGURATION GUIDE

CONFIGURING PRODUCT INFORMATION MANAGEMENT WITHIN DYNAMICS 365 FOR OPERATIONS
MODULE 1: CONFIGURING THE PRODUCT INFORMATION MANAGEMENT CONTROLS

Creating a Serial Number Tracking Dimension Group

How to do it...

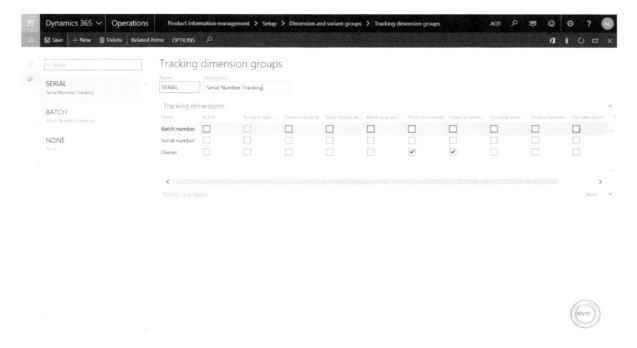

Step 4: Save the Tracking dimension group

Now we will want to save the new **Tracking dimension group** record.

To do this, we just need to click on the **Save** button in the menu bar.

After you have done that you will notice that the tracking dimension levels will be populated with different flags to manage how you track the tracking dimensions.

www.dynamicscompanions.com
Dynamics Companions

- 69 -

www.blindsquirrelpublishing.com
© 2017 Blind Squirrel Publishing, LLC , All Rights Reserved

BLIND SQUIRREL
PUBLISHING

DYNAMICS COMPANIONS
BARE BONES CONFIGURATION GUIDE

CONFIGURING PRODUCT INFORMATION MANAGEMENT WITHIN DYNAMICS 365 FOR OPERATIONS
MODULE 1: CONFIGURING THE PRODUCT INFORMATION MANAGEMENT CONTROLS

Creating a Serial Number Tracking Dimension Group

How to do it...

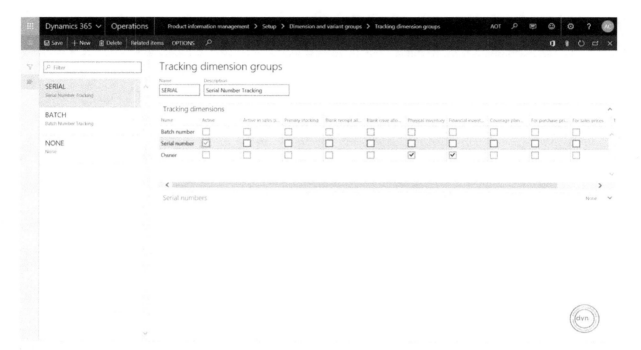

Step 5: Make Serial tracking active

Now we will want to activate **Serial number** tracking on our **Tracking dimension group**.

To do this we just need to toggle the **Active** flag on the **Serial number** tracking dimension.

For this **Tracking dimension group**, we want just the serial number tracking to be enabled, so we will want to check the **Active** flag within the **Serial number** tracking dimension line.

www.dynamicscompanions.com
Dynamics Companions

- 70 -

www.blindsquirrelpublishing.com
© 2017 Blind Squirrel Publishing, LLC , All Rights Reserved

BLIND SQUIRREL
PUBLISHING

DYNAMICS COMPANIONS
BARE BONES CONFIGURATION GUIDE

CONFIGURING PRODUCT INFORMATION MANAGEMENT WITHIN DYNAMICS 365 FOR OPERATIONS
MODULE 1: CONFIGURING THE PRODUCT INFORMATION MANAGEMENT CONTROLS

Creating a Serial Number Tracking Dimension Group

How to do it...

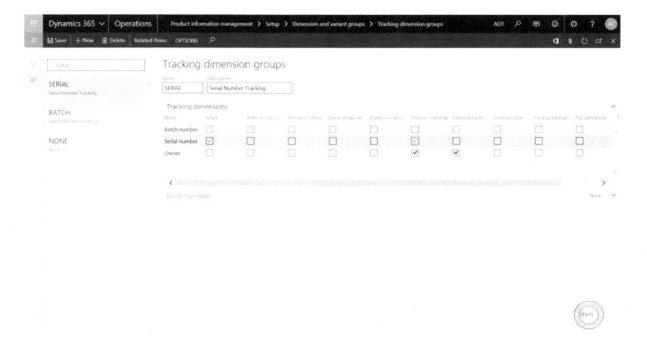

Step 6: Mark Physical Inventory to be tracked by Serial number

Before we are finish we will need to make one final change and that is to mark the inventory as being tracked at the serial number.

To do this we will just want to toggle the **Physical Inventory** flag at the **Serial number** tracking dimension.

For this **Tracking dimension group**, we want the inventory to be tracked at the serial number level, so we will want to check the **Physical inventory** flag within the **Serial number** tracking dimension line.

www.dynamicscompanions.com
Dynamics Companions

- 71 -

www.blindsquirrelpublishing.com
© 2017 Blind Squirrel Publishing, LLC , All Rights Reserved

BLIND SQUIRREL
PUBLISHING

DYNAMICS COMPANIONS
BARE BONES CONFIGURATION GUIDE

CONFIGURING PRODUCT INFORMATION MANAGEMENT WITHIN DYNAMICS 365 FOR OPERATIONS
MODULE 1: CONFIGURING THE PRODUCT INFORMATION MANAGEMENT CONTROLS

Creating a Batch and Serial Number Tracking Dimension Group

The final **Tracking dimension group** that we will configure is one that will allow us to mark a product to be tracked by both their **Batch** and **Serial number**.

We will use this type of **Tracking dimension group** to track products that may be produced together within a manufacturing run, which we also want to track individually through traces.

An example of the type of product that may use this tracking dimension group could be products that are produced and then placed in individual boxes that need to be tracked.

How to do it...

Step 1: Create a new Tracking dimension group

We will now want to create our final **Tracking dimension group** record.

Click on the **New** button

Step 2: Give the Tracking dimension group a Name

Now we will want to give our **Tracking dimension group** a code that we will be able to use as a reference.

Set the **Name** to BATCHSER

Step 3: Add a Description to the Tracking dimension group

Next we will want to add a **Description** to the **Tracking dimension group** that is a little more descriptive for the users.

Set the Description to Batch & Serial Number Tracking

Step 4: Save the Tracking dimension group

Now we will want to save the new **Tracking dimension group** record.

Click on the **Save** button

Step 5: Expand the Serial numbers tab

Before we continue on we will want to make one quick configuration change to enable serial number control.

Expand the **Serial numbers** tab

Step 6: Enable Serial number control

This will allow us to see a few additional controls that we can configure for the tracking dimension group that are related to serial number tracking.

Now we will want to enable Serial number control.

Set the Serial number control to Yes

dync
www.dynamicscompanions.com
Dynamics Companions

- 72 -

www.blindsquirrelpublishing.com
© 2017 Blind Squirrel Publishing, LLC , All Rights Reserved

BLIND SQUIRREL
PUBLISHING

DYNAMICS COMPANIONS
BARE BONES CONFIGURATION GUIDE

CONFIGURING PRODUCT INFORMATION MANAGEMENT WITHIN DYNAMICS 365 FOR OPERATIONS
MODULE 1: CONFIGURING THE PRODUCT INFORMATION MANAGEMENT CONTROLS

Step 7: Make Batch tracking active

Now we will want to activate **Batch number** tracking on our **Tracking dimension group**.

Check the Batch number Active flag

Step 8: Make Serial tracking active

Now we will want to activate **Serial number** tracking on our **Tracking dimension group**.

Check the Serial number Active flag

Step 9: Mark Physical Inventory to be tracked by Batch

Now we will need to make one final change and that is to mark the inventory as being tracked at the batch number.

Check the Batch number Physical Inventory flag

Step 10: Mark Physical Inventory to be tracked by Serial number

Before we are finish we will need to make one final change and that is to mark the inventory as being tracked at the serial number.

Check the Serial number Physical Inventory flag

www.dynamicscompanions.com
Dynamics Companions

- 73 -

www.blindsquirrelpublishing.com
© 2017 Blind Squirrel Publishing, LLC , All Rights Reserved

BLIND SQUIRREL
PUBLISHING

DYNAMICS COMPANIONS
BARE BONES CONFIGURATION GUIDE

CONFIGURING PRODUCT INFORMATION MANAGEMENT WITHIN DYNAMICS 365 FOR OPERATIONS
MODULE 1: CONFIGURING THE PRODUCT INFORMATION MANAGEMENT CONTROLS

Creating a Batch and Serial Number Tracking Dimension Group

How to do it...

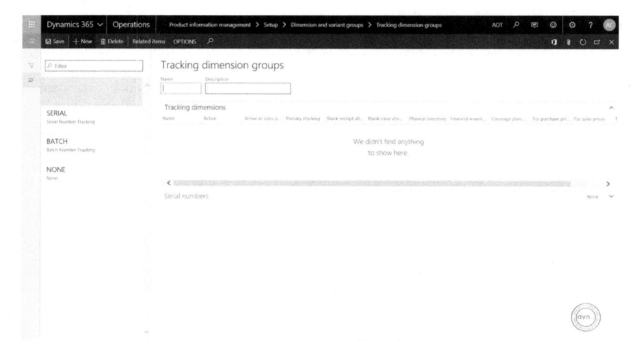

Step 1: Create a new Tracking dimension group

We will now want to create our final **Tracking dimension group** record.

To do this, all we need to do is click on the **New** button in the menu bar and this will create a new record for us.

www.dynamicscompanions.com
Dynamics Companions

- 74 -

www.blindsquirrelpublishing.com
© 2017 Blind Squirrel Publishing, LLC , All Rights Reserved

BLIND SQUIRREL
PUBLISHING

DYNAMICS COMPANIONS
BARE BONES CONFIGURATION GUIDE

CONFIGURING PRODUCT INFORMATION MANAGEMENT WITHIN DYNAMICS 365 FOR OPERATIONS
MODULE 1: CONFIGURING THE PRODUCT INFORMATION MANAGEMENT CONTROLS

Creating a Batch and Serial Number Tracking Dimension Group

How to do it...

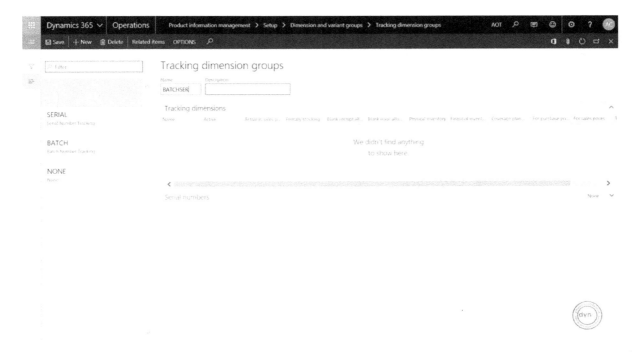

Step 2: Give the Tracking dimension group a Name

Now we will want to give our **Tracking dimension group** a code that we will be able to use as a reference.

To do this we just type in the code that we want to assign to the **Tracking dimension group** into the **Name** field.

For this **Tracking dimension group,** since we will be using this to identify products that are tracked by their batch and serial number we will set the **Name** to **BATCHSER**.

dyn

www.dynamicscompanions.com
Dynamics Companions

- 75 -

www.blindsquirrelpublishing.com
© 2017 Blind Squirrel Publishing, LLC, All Rights Reserved

BLIND SQUIRREL
PUBLISHING

DYNAMICS COMPANIONS
BARE BONES CONFIGURATION GUIDE

CONFIGURING PRODUCT INFORMATION MANAGEMENT WITHIN DYNAMICS 365 FOR OPERATIONS
MODULE 1: CONFIGURING THE PRODUCT INFORMATION MANAGEMENT CONTROLS

Creating a Batch and Serial Number Tracking Dimension Group

How to do it...

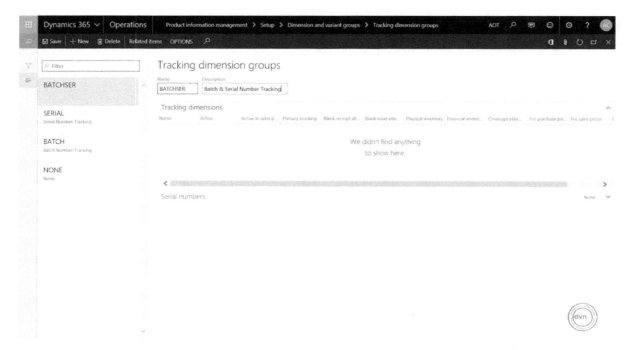

Step 3: Add a Description to the Tracking dimension group

Next we will want to add a **Description** to the **Tracking dimension group** that is a little more descriptive for the users.

To do this we just need to type in the description of the **Tracking dimension group** into the **Description** field.

For this Tracking dimension group we will set the Description to Serial Number Tracking to match the Name.

dync
www.dynamicscompanions.com
Dynamics Companions

- 76 -

www.blindsquirrelpublishing.com
© 2017 Blind Squirrel Publishing, LLC , All Rights Reserved

BLIND SQUIRREL
PUBLISHING

DYNAMICS COMPANIONS
BARE BONES CONFIGURATION GUIDE

CONFIGURING PRODUCT INFORMATION MANAGEMENT WITHIN DYNAMICS 365 FOR OPERATIONS
MODULE 1: CONFIGURING THE PRODUCT INFORMATION MANAGEMENT CONTROLS

Creating a Batch and Serial Number Tracking Dimension Group

How to do it...

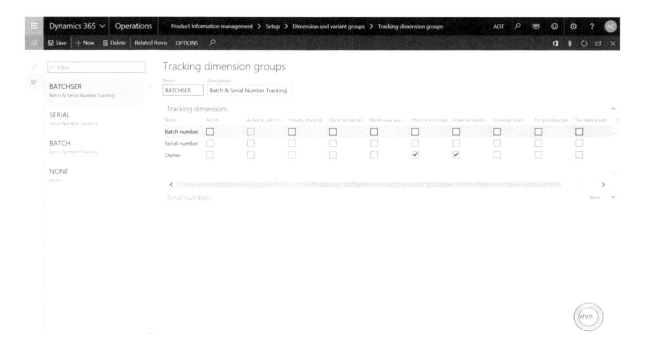

Step 4: Save the Tracking dimension group

Now we will want to save the new **Tracking dimension group** record.

To do this, we just need to click on the **Save** button in the menu bar.

After you have done that you will notice that the tracking dimension levels will be populated with different flags to manage how you track the tracking dimensions.

www.dynamicscompanions.com
Dynamics Companions

- 77 -

www.blindsquirrelpublishing.com
© 2017 Blind Squirrel Publishing, LLC , All Rights Reserved

BLIND SQUIRREL
PUBLISHING

DYNAMICS COMPANIONS
BARE BONES CONFIGURATION GUIDE

CONFIGURING PRODUCT INFORMATION MANAGEMENT WITHIN DYNAMICS 365 FOR OPERATIONS
MODULE 1: CONFIGURING THE PRODUCT INFORMATION MANAGEMENT CONTROLS

Creating a Batch and Serial Number Tracking Dimension Group

How to do it...

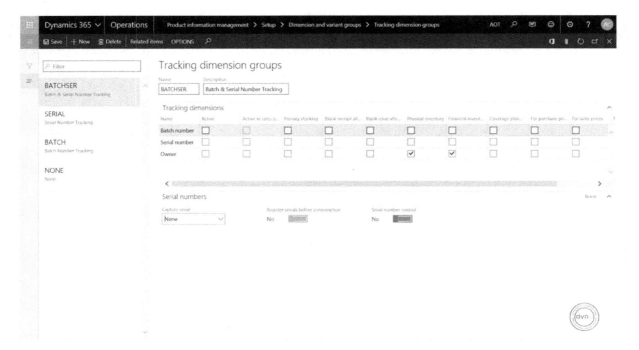

Step 5: Expand the Serial numbers tab

Before we continue on we will want to make one quick configuration change to enable serial number control.

To so this we will start off by expanding the **Serial numbers** tab group at the bottom of the form.

www.dynamicscompanions.com
Dynamics Companions

- 78 -

www.blindsquirrelpublishing.com
© 2017 Blind Squirrel Publishing, LLC, All Rights Reserved

BLIND SQUIRREL
PUBLISHING

DYNAMICS COMPANIONS
BARE BONES CONFIGURATION GUIDE

CONFIGURING PRODUCT INFORMATION MANAGEMENT WITHIN DYNAMICS 365 FOR OPERATIONS
MODULE 1: CONFIGURING THE PRODUCT INFORMATION MANAGEMENT CONTROLS

Creating a Batch and Serial Number Tracking Dimension Group

How to do it...

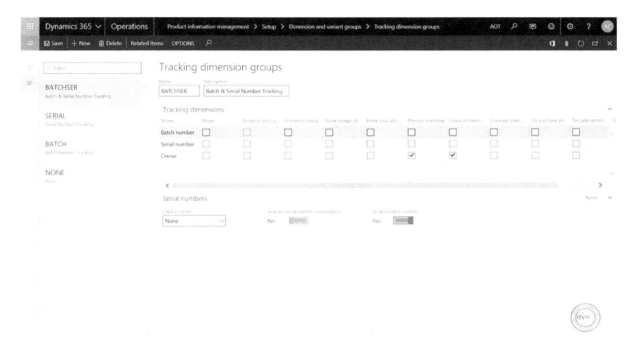

Step 6: Enable Serial number control

This will allow us to see a few additional controls that we can configure for the tracking dimension group that are related to serial number tracking.

Now we will want to enable Serial number control.

To do this we just toggle the **Serial number control** switch.

For this tracking dimension group we will want to add additional control on the serial numbers so we will want to set the **Serial number control** switch to **Yes**.

www.dynamicscompanions.com
Dynamics Companions

- 79 -

www.blindsquirrelpublishing.com
© 2017 Blind Squirrel Publishing, LLC, All Rights Reserved

BLIND SQUIRREL
PUBLISHING

DYNAMICS COMPANIONS
BARE BONES CONFIGURATION GUIDE

CONFIGURING PRODUCT INFORMATION MANAGEMENT WITHIN DYNAMICS 365 FOR OPERATIONS
MODULE 1: CONFIGURING THE PRODUCT INFORMATION MANAGEMENT CONTROLS

Creating a Batch and Serial Number Tracking Dimension Group

How to do it...

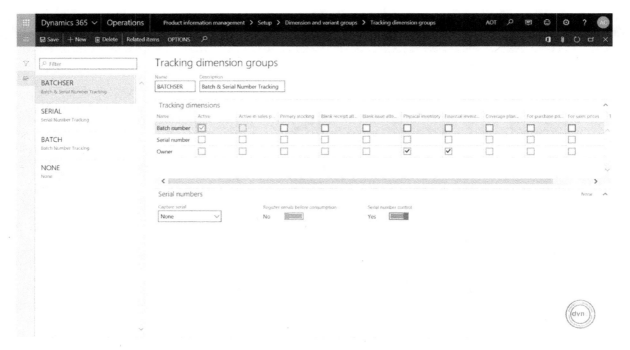

Step 7: Make Batch tracking active

Now we will want to activate **Batch number** tracking on our **Tracking dimension group**.

To do this we just need to toggle the **Active** flag on the **Batch number** tracking dimension.

For this **Tracking dimension group**, we want just the batch number tracking to be enabled, so we will want to check the **Active** flag within the **Batch number** tracking dimension line.

DYNAMICS COMPANIONS
BARE BONES CONFIGURATION GUIDE

CONFIGURING PRODUCT INFORMATION MANAGEMENT WITHIN DYNAMICS 365 FOR OPERATIONS
MODULE 1: CONFIGURING THE PRODUCT INFORMATION MANAGEMENT CONTROLS

Creating a Batch and Serial Number Tracking Dimension Group

How to do it...

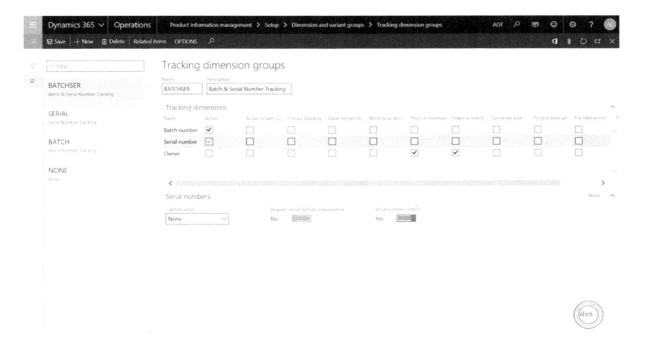

Step 8: Make Serial tracking active

Now we will want to activate **Serial number** tracking on our **Tracking dimension group**.

To do this we just need to toggle the **Active** flag on the **Serial number** tracking dimension.

For this **Tracking dimension group**, we want just the serial number tracking to be enabled, so we will want to check the **Active** flag within the **Serial number** tracking dimension line.

www.dynamicscompanions.com
Dynamics Companions

- 81 -

www.blindsquirrelpublishing.com
© 2017 Blind Squirrel Publishing, LLC , All Rights Reserved

BLIND SQUIRREL
PUBLISHING

DYNAMICS COMPANIONS
BARE BONES CONFIGURATION GUIDE

CONFIGURING PRODUCT INFORMATION MANAGEMENT WITHIN DYNAMICS 365 FOR OPERATIONS
MODULE 1: CONFIGURING THE PRODUCT INFORMATION MANAGEMENT CONTROLS

Creating a Batch and Serial Number Tracking Dimension Group

How to do it...

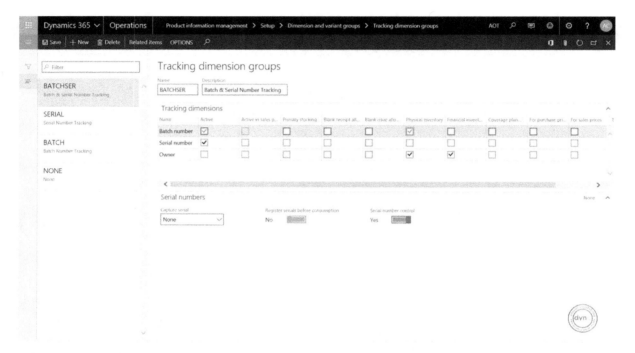

Step 9: Mark Physical Inventory to be tracked by Batch

Now we will need to make one final change and that is to mark the inventory as being tracked at the batch number.

To do this we will just want to toggle the **Physical Inventory** flag at the **Batch Number** tracking dimension.

For this **Tracking dimension group**, we want the inventory to be tracked at the batch number level, so we will want to check the **Physical inventory** flag within the **Batch number** tracking dimension line.

www.dynamicscompanions.com
Dynamics Companions

- 82 -

www.blindsquirrelpublishing.com
© 2017 Blind Squirrel Publishing, LLC , All Rights Reserved

BLIND SQUIRREL
PUBLISHING

DYNAMICS COMPANIONS
BARE BONES CONFIGURATION GUIDE

CONFIGURING PRODUCT INFORMATION MANAGEMENT WITHIN DYNAMICS 365 FOR OPERATIONS
MODULE 1: CONFIGURING THE PRODUCT INFORMATION MANAGEMENT CONTROLS

Creating a Batch and Serial Number Tracking Dimension Group

How to do it...

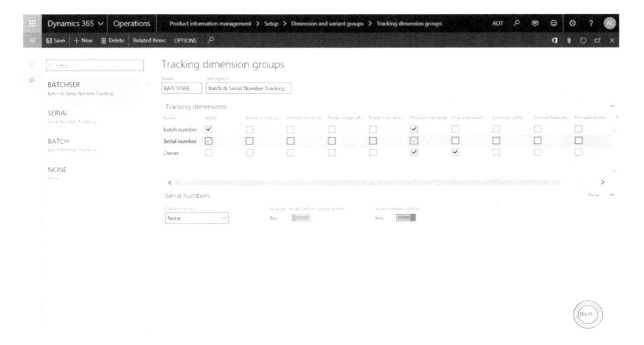

Step 10: Mark Physical Inventory to be tracked by Serial number

Before we are finish we will need to make one final change and that is to mark the inventory as being tracked at the serial number.

To do this we will just want to toggle the **Physical Inventory** flag at the **Serial number** tracking dimension.

For this **Tracking dimension group**, we want the inventory to be tracked at the serial number level, so we will want to check the **Physical inventory** flag within the **Serial number** tracking dimension line.

dyn

www.dynamicscompanions.com
Dynamics Companions

- 83 -

www.blindsquirrelpublishing.com
© 2017 Blind Squirrel Publishing, LLC, All Rights Reserved

BLIND SQUIRREL
PUBLISHING

DYNAMICS COMPANIONS
BARE BONES CONFIGURATION GUIDE

CONFIGURING PRODUCT INFORMATION MANAGEMENT WITHIN DYNAMICS 365 FOR OPERATIONS
MODULE 1: CONFIGURING THE PRODUCT INFORMATION MANAGEMENT CONTROLS

Summary

Now we have all of the main types of Inventory Tracking Dimensions configured. We have a way that we can track the products by **Batch**, by **Seral Number**, by both, and even not at all.

DYNAMICS COMPANIONS
BARE BONES CONFIGURATION GUIDE

CONFIGURING PRODUCT INFORMATION MANAGEMENT WITHIN DYNAMICS 365 FOR OPERATIONS
MODULE 1: CONFIGURING THE PRODUCT INFORMATION MANAGEMENT CONTROLS

Configuring the Units Of Measure

Although Dynamics 365 is preconfigured with a whole slew of default **Units of Measures**, there will probably be some additional ones that are specific to our products that are not part of the standard data. So before we start setting up our products, we will want to quickly set up the standard **Units Of Measures** and then a few more for good measure.

Topics Covered

Opening the Units form

Using the Unit Creation Wizard

Creating a new Quantity based Unit

Creating a Time based Unit

Creating an Electric Charge based Unit

Summary

www.dynamicscompanions.com
Dynamics Companions

- 85 -

www.blindsquirrelpublishing.com
© 2017 Blind Squirrel Publishing, LLC , All Rights Reserved

BLIND SQUIRREL
PUBLISHING

DYNAMICS COMPANIONS
BARE BONES CONFIGURATION GUIDE

CONFIGURING PRODUCT INFORMATION MANAGEMENT WITHIN DYNAMICS 365 FOR OPERATIONS
MODULE 1: CONFIGURING THE PRODUCT INFORMATION MANAGEMENT CONTROLS

Opening the Units form

To do this we will want to open the **Units** maintenance form which will allow us to configure all of the different units of measure that we will be able to measure and count our products by.

How to do it...

Step 1: Open the Units form through the menu

We can get to the **Units** form a couple of different ways. The first way is through the master menu.

Navigate to Organization administration > Setup > Units > Unite

Step 2: Open the Units form through the menu search

Another way that we can find the **Units** form is through the menu search feature.

Type in **units** into the menu search and select **Units**

www.dynamicscompanions.com
Dynamics Companions

- 86 -

www.blindsquirrelpublishing.com
© 2017 Blind Squirrel Publishing, LLC , All Rights Reserved

BLIND SQUIRREL
PUBLISHING

DYNAMICS COMPANIONS
BARE BONES CONFIGURATION GUIDE

CONFIGURING PRODUCT INFORMATION MANAGEMENT WITHIN DYNAMICS 365 FOR OPERATIONS
MODULE 1: CONFIGURING THE PRODUCT INFORMATION MANAGEMENT CONTROLS

Opening the Units form

How to do it...

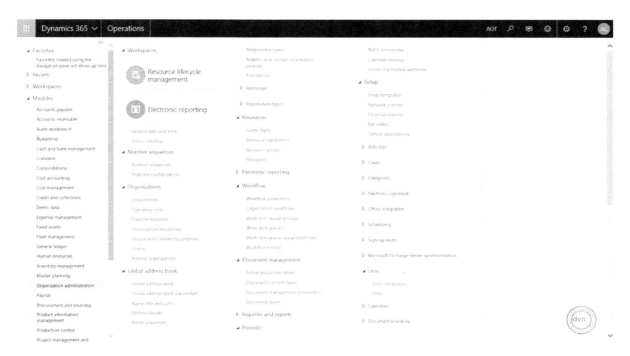

Step 1: Open the Units form through the menu

We can get to the **Units** form a couple of different ways. The first way is through the master menu.

To do this, click on the **Units** menu item within the **Units** subgroup of the **Setup** group within the **Organization Administration** area page.

dyn c
www.dynamicscompanions.com
Dynamics Companions

- 87 -

www.blindsquirrelpublishing.com
© 2017 Blind Squirrel Publishing, LLC , All Rights Reserved

BLIND SQUIRREL
PUBLISHING

DYNAMICS COMPANIONS
BARE BONES CONFIGURATION GUIDE

CONFIGURING PRODUCT INFORMATION MANAGEMENT WITHIN DYNAMICS 365 FOR OPERATIONS
MODULE 1: CONFIGURING THE PRODUCT INFORMATION MANAGEMENT CONTROLS

Opening the Units form

How to do it...

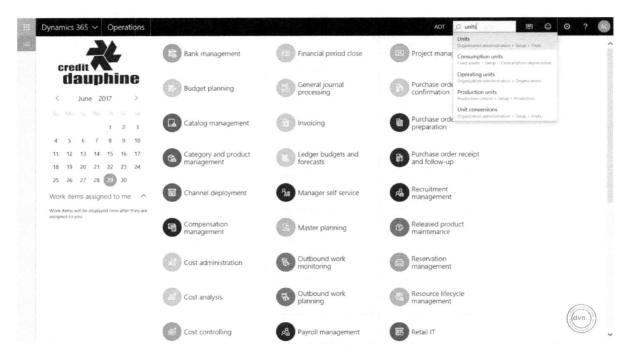

Step 2: Open the Units form through the menu search

Another way that we can find the **Units** form is through the menu search feature.

We can do this by clicking on the search icon in the header of the form (or by pressing **ALT+G**) and then typing in **units** into the search box. Then you will be able to select the **Units** maintenance form from the dropdown list.

dync
www.dynamicscompanions.com
Dynamics Companions

- 88 -

www.blindsquirrelpublishing.com
© 2017 Blind Squirrel Publishing, LLC , All Rights Reserved

BLIND SQUIRREL
PUBLISHING

DYNAMICS COMPANIONS
BARE BONES CONFIGURATION GUIDE

CONFIGURING PRODUCT INFORMATION MANAGEMENT WITHIN DYNAMICS 365 FOR OPERATIONS
MODULE 1: CONFIGURING THE PRODUCT INFORMATION MANAGEMENT CONTROLS

Opening the Units form

How to do it...

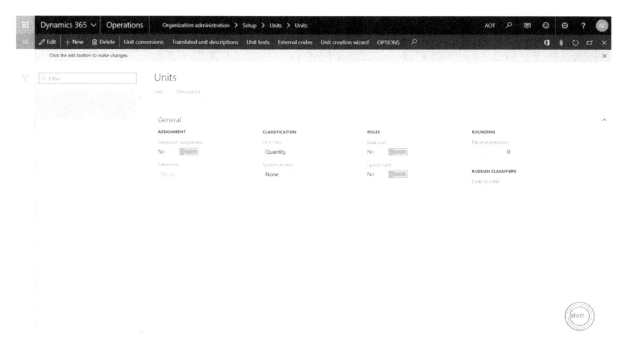

Step 2: Open the Units form through the menu search

This will open up the **Units** maintenance form where we will be able to define all of the different units of measure that we want to use.

www.dynamicscompanions.com
Dynamics Companions

- 89 -

www.blindsquirrelpublishing.com
© 2017 Blind Squirrel Publishing, LLC , All Rights Reserved

BLIND SQUIRREL
PUBLISHING

DYNAMICS COMPANIONS
BARE BONES CONFIGURATION GUIDE

CONFIGURING PRODUCT INFORMATION MANAGEMENT WITHIN DYNAMICS 365 FOR OPERATIONS
MODULE 1: CONFIGURING THE PRODUCT INFORMATION MANAGEMENT CONTROLS

Using the Unit Creation Wizard

Now we can start to set up all of the **Units** that we will want to use within our company. But, we don't have to set up all of the units of measures by hand. There is a wizard that we can take advantage of that will save ourselves a little bit of time, and have Dynamics 365 create all of the most common **Units** and also **Unit Conversions** for us.

How to do it...

Step 1: Start the Unit creation wizard

All we need to do is start the unit creation wizard.

Click on the **Unit creation wizard** menu item

Step 2: Click Next

This will kick off the **Unit Setup** wizard.

From here we can select the types of Units that we want to set up, like Imperial or Metric units, and also if we want to create the conversion factors as well.

We want to create all of the **Units.**

Click on the **Next** button

Step 3: Click Next

Next we will see a list of all of the **Units** that Dynamics 365 is proposing to create for us.

From here we can remove any **Unit** that we don't want to create.

On this step we want to create all of the suggested **Units.**

Click on the **Next** button.

Step 4: Click Next

Next we will see a list of all of the **Unit conversions** that Dynamics 365 is proposing to create for us.

Just like on the **Units** page, here we can remove any **Unit conversion** that we don't want to create.

Here we want to keep all of the standard conversion factors.

Click on the **Next** button

Step 5: Click Finish

Now we will be taken to the last page where we will be able to see all of the **Unit** records that Dynamics 365 is about to create for us.

All we need to do now is start the process of creating the standard **Units** and **Unit conversion** records.

Click on the **Finish** button.

When we return back to the **Units** maintenance form we will see that all of the default **Units** and also their **Unit conversion** factors g=have been set up for us.

www.dynamicscompanions.com
Dynamics Companions

- 90 -

www.blindsquirrelpublishing.com
© 2017 Blind Squirrel Publishing, LLC , All Rights Reserved

BLIND SQUIRREL
PUBLISHING

DYNAMICS COMPANIONS
BARE BONES CONFIGURATION GUIDE

CONFIGURING PRODUCT INFORMATION MANAGEMENT WITHIN DYNAMICS 365 FOR OPERATIONS
MODULE 1: CONFIGURING THE PRODUCT INFORMATION MANAGEMENT CONTROLS

Using the Unit Creation Wizard

How to do it...

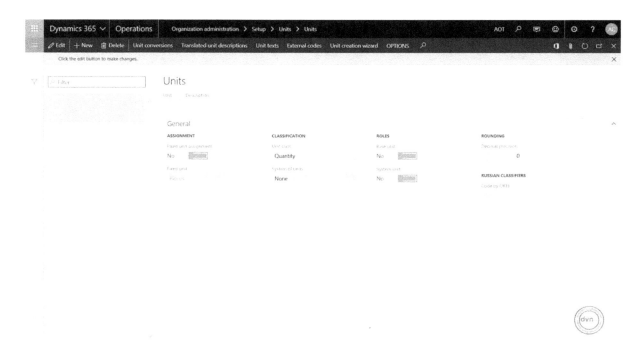

Step 1: Start the Unit creation wizard

All we need to do is start the unit creation wizard.

To do this just click on the **Unit creation wizard** menu item within the menu bar.

www.dynamicscompanions.com
Dynamics Companions

- 91 -

www.blindsquirrelpublishing.com
© 2017 Blind Squirrel Publishing, LLC , All Rights Reserved

BLIND SQUIRREL
PUBLISHING

DYNAMICS COMPANIONS
BARE BONES CONFIGURATION GUIDE

CONFIGURING PRODUCT INFORMATION MANAGEMENT WITHIN DYNAMICS 365 FOR OPERATIONS
MODULE 1: CONFIGURING THE PRODUCT INFORMATION MANAGEMENT CONTROLS

Using the Unit Creation Wizard

How to do it...

Step 2: Click Next

This will kick off the **Unit Setup** wizard.

From here we can select the types of Units that we want to set up, like Imperial or Metric units, and also if we want to create the conversion factors as well.

We want to create all of the **Units.**

To do this, just leave all the defaults as they are and click on the **Next** button.

dyn c
www.dynamicscompanions.com
Dynamics Companions

- 92 -

www.blindsquirrelpublishing.com
© 2017 Blind Squirrel Publishing, LLC , All Rights Reserved

BLIND SQUIRREL
PUBLISHING

DYNAMICS COMPANIONS
BARE BONES CONFIGURATION GUIDE

CONFIGURING PRODUCT INFORMATION MANAGEMENT WITHIN DYNAMICS 365 FOR OPERATIONS
MODULE 1: CONFIGURING THE PRODUCT INFORMATION MANAGEMENT CONTROLS

Using the Unit Creation Wizard

How to do it...

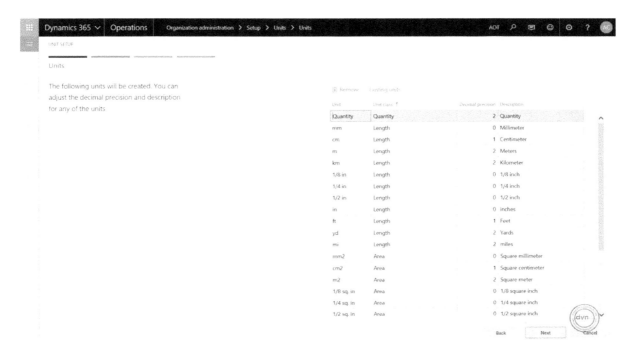

Step 3: Click Next

Next we will see a list of all of the **Units** that Dynamics 365 is proposing to create for us.

From here we can remove any **Unit** that we don't want to create.

On this step we want to create all of the suggested **Units.**

To do this, we will just leave all of the suggested **Units** as they are and click on the **Next** button.

dyn c
www.dynamicscompanions.com
Dynamics Companions

- 93 -

www.blindsquirrelpublishing.com
© 2017 Blind Squirrel Publishing, LLC , All Rights Reserved

BLIND SQUIRREL
PUBLISHING

DYNAMICS COMPANIONS
BARE BONES CONFIGURATION GUIDE

CONFIGURING PRODUCT INFORMATION MANAGEMENT WITHIN DYNAMICS 365 FOR OPERATIONS
MODULE 1: CONFIGURING THE PRODUCT INFORMATION MANAGEMENT CONTROLS

Using the Unit Creation Wizard

How to do it...

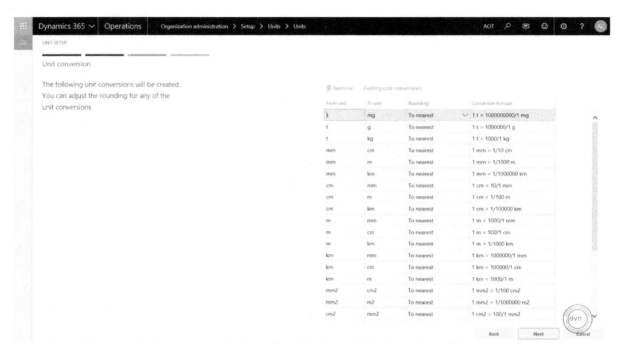

Step 4: Click Next

Next we will see a list of all of the **Unit conversions** that Dynamics 365 is proposing to create for us.

Just like on the **Units** page, here we can remove any **Unit conversion** that we don't want to create.

Here we want to keep all of the standard conversion factors.

To do this, we will just leave all of the suggested **Unit conversions** as they are and click on the **Next** button.

www.dynamicscompanions.com
Dynamics Companions

- 94 -

www.blindsquirrelpublishing.com
© 2017 Blind Squirrel Publishing, LLC , All Rights Reserved

BLIND SQUIRREL
PUBLISHING

DYNAMICS COMPANIONS
BARE BONES CONFIGURATION GUIDE

CONFIGURING PRODUCT INFORMATION MANAGEMENT WITHIN DYNAMICS 365 FOR OPERATIONS
MODULE 1: CONFIGURING THE PRODUCT INFORMATION MANAGEMENT CONTROLS

Using the Unit Creation Wizard

How to do it...

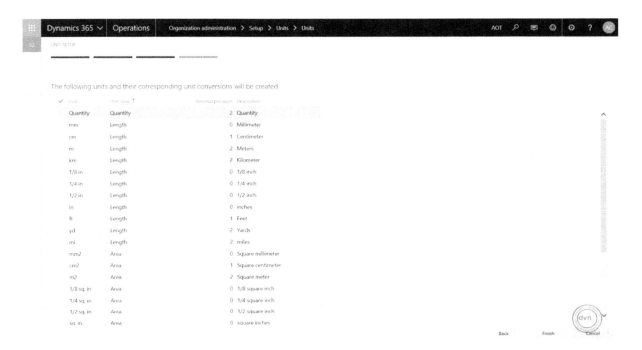

Step 5: Click Finish

Now we will be taken to the last page where we will be able to see all of the **Unit** records that Dynamics 365 is about to create for us.

All we need to do now is start the process of creating the standard **Units** and **Unit conversion** records.

To do this we just have to click on the **Finish** button.

www.dynamicscompanions.com
Dynamics Companions

- 95 -

www.blindsquirrelpublishing.com
© 2017 Blind Squirrel Publishing, LLC , All Rights Reserved

BLIND SQUIRREL
PUBLISHING

DYNAMICS COMPANIONS
BARE BONES CONFIGURATION GUIDE

CONFIGURING PRODUCT INFORMATION MANAGEMENT WITHIN DYNAMICS 365 FOR OPERATIONS
MODULE 1: CONFIGURING THE PRODUCT INFORMATION MANAGEMENT CONTROLS

Using the Unit Creation Wizard

How to do it...

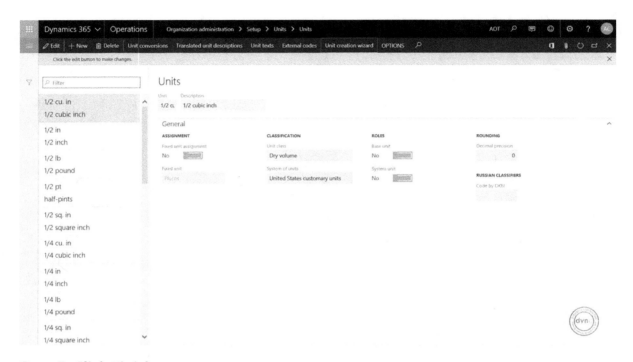

Step 5: Click Finish

When we return back to the **Units** maintenance form we will see that all of the default **Units** and also their **Unit conversion** factors g=have been set up for us.

www.dynamicscompanions.com
Dynamics Companions

- 96 -

www.blindsquirrelpublishing.com
© 2017 Blind Squirrel Publishing, LLC , All Rights Reserved

BLIND SQUIRREL
PUBLISHING

DYNAMICS COMPANIONS
BARE BONES CONFIGURATION GUIDE

CONFIGURING PRODUCT INFORMATION MANAGEMENT WITHIN DYNAMICS 365 FOR OPERATIONS
MODULE 1: CONFIGURING THE PRODUCT INFORMATION MANAGEMENT CONTROLS

Creating a new Quantity based Unit

Dynamics 365 will create all of the usual **Units of Measure** for us, but not all of the ones that we may want to use. If there are any **Units** that are missing then we can easily add them in alongside the standard ones.

How to do it...

Step 1: Click New

We will be tracking a lot of our products as eaches, which is not one of the units that are created by the wizard. So we will want to create a new **Unit** to track the individual each count.

We will start off by creating a new **Unit** record.

Click on the **New** button.

Step 2: Update the Unit

Now that we have a new record we will want to assign an identifier for the Unit that we will use everywhere in the system as the Unit code.

Set the **Unit** to **ea**

Step 3: Update Description

Next we will want to add a more detailed description of the **Unit** that we can use within reporting, and also to give the user a better description of the unit code.

Set the Description to Each

Step 4: Select the Unit class

Each **Unit** can be assigned to a specific **Unit class** which indicates the type of unit that this is and what it measures.

If you click on the **Unit Class** you will be able to see that there are a number of different classifications that you can assign to your **Unit**.

Click on the **Unit class** dropdown list and select **Quantity**

Once we have done that, our **Unit** is configured.

www.dynamicscompanions.com
Dynamics Companions

- 97 -

www.blindsquirrelpublishing.com
© 2017 Blind Squirrel Publishing, LLC , All Rights Reserved

BLIND SQUIRREL
PUBLISHING

DYNAMICS COMPANIONS
BARE BONES CONFIGURATION GUIDE

CONFIGURING PRODUCT INFORMATION MANAGEMENT WITHIN DYNAMICS 365 FOR OPERATIONS
MODULE 1: CONFIGURING THE PRODUCT INFORMATION MANAGEMENT CONTROLS

Creating a new Quantity based Unit

How to do it...

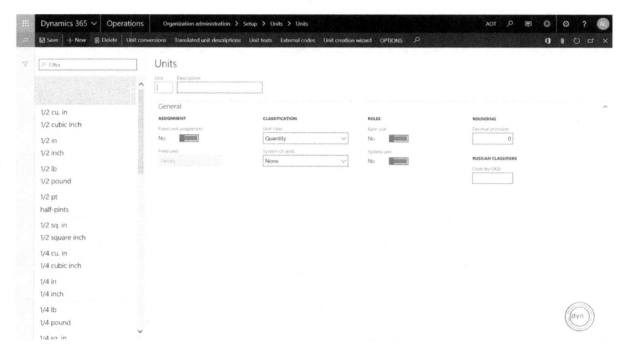

Step 1: Click New

We will be tracking a lot of our products as eaches, which is not one of the units that are created by the wizard. So we will want to create a new **Unit** to track the individual each count.

We will start off by creating a new **Unit** record.

To do this just click on the **New** button in the menu bar.

dync
www.dynamicscompanions.com
Dynamics Companions

- 98 -

www.blindsquirrelpublishing.com
© 2017 Blind Squirrel Publishing, LLC, All Rights Reserved

BLIND SQUIRREL
PUBLISHING

DYNAMICS COMPANIONS
BARE BONES CONFIGURATION GUIDE

CONFIGURING PRODUCT INFORMATION MANAGEMENT WITHIN DYNAMICS 365 FOR OPERATIONS
MODULE 1: CONFIGURING THE PRODUCT INFORMATION MANAGEMENT CONTROLS

Creating a new Quantity based Unit

How to do it...

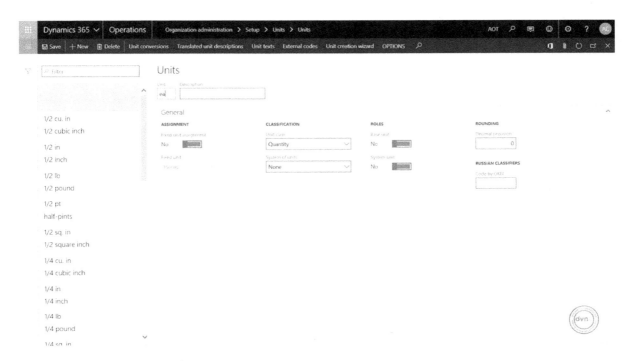

Step 2: Update the Unit

Now that we have a new record we will want to assign an identifier for the Unit that we will use everywhere in the system as the Unit code.

To do this we will just need to type in the **Unit** value.

For this example, we will want to set the **Unit** to **ea**.

www.dynamicscompanions.com
Dynamics Companions

- 99 -

www.blindsquirrelpublishing.com
© 2017 Blind Squirrel Publishing, LLC, All Rights Reserved

BLIND SQUIRREL
PUBLISHING

DYNAMICS COMPANIONS
BARE BONES CONFIGURATION GUIDE

CONFIGURING PRODUCT INFORMATION MANAGEMENT WITHIN DYNAMICS 365 FOR OPERATIONS
MODULE 1: CONFIGURING THE PRODUCT INFORMATION MANAGEMENT CONTROLS

Creating a new Quantity based Unit

How to do it...

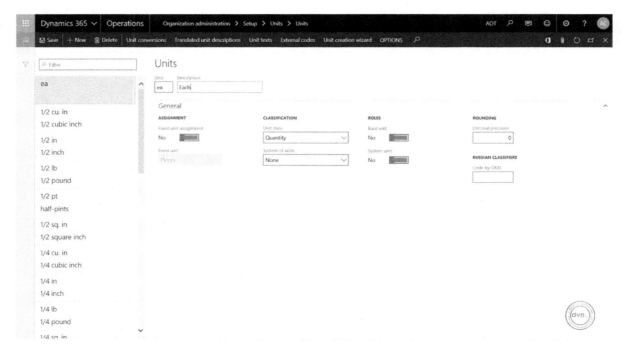

Step 3: Update Description

Next we will want to add a more detailed description of the **Unit** that we can use within reporting, and also to give the user a better description of the unit code.

To do this we will just need to type in the **Description** value.

For this example, we will want to set the **Description** to **Each**.

dync

www.dynamicscompanions.com
Dynamics Companions

- 100 -

www.blindsquirrelpublishing.com
© 2017 Blind Squirrel Publishing, LLC , All Rights Reserved

BLIND SQUIRREL
PUBLISHING

DYNAMICS COMPANIONS
BARE BONES CONFIGURATION GUIDE

CONFIGURING PRODUCT INFORMATION MANAGEMENT WITHIN DYNAMICS 365 FOR OPERATIONS
MODULE 1: CONFIGURING THE PRODUCT INFORMATION MANAGEMENT CONTROLS

Creating a new Quantity based Unit

How to do it...

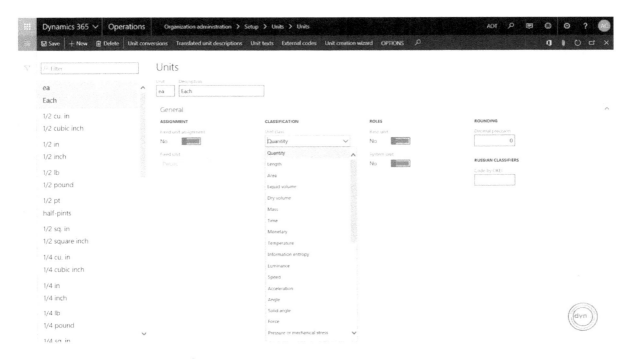

Step 4: Select the Unit class

Each **Unit** can be assigned to a specific **Unit class** which indicates the type of unit that this is and what it measures.

If you click on the **Unit Class** you will be able to see that there are a number of different classifications that you can assign to your **Unit**.

To do this we will just need to select the **Unit class** from the dropdown list.

For this example, we will want to click on the **Unit class** dropdown list and select **Quantity**.

dyn c

www.dynamicscompanions.com
Dynamics Companions

- 101 -

www.blindsquirrelpublishing.com
© 2017 Blind Squirrel Publishing, LLC , All Rights Reserved

BLIND SQUIRREL
PUBLISHING

DYNAMICS COMPANIONS
BARE BONES CONFIGURATION GUIDE

CONFIGURING PRODUCT INFORMATION MANAGEMENT WITHIN DYNAMICS 365 FOR OPERATIONS
MODULE 1: CONFIGURING THE PRODUCT INFORMATION MANAGEMENT CONTROLS

Creating a new Quantity based Unit

How to do it...

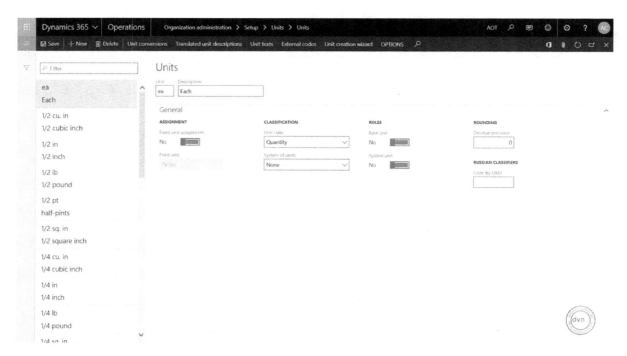

Step 4: Select the Unit class

Once we have done that, our **Unit** is configured.

DYNAMICS COMPANIONS
BARE BONES CONFIGURATION GUIDE

CONFIGURING PRODUCT INFORMATION MANAGEMENT WITHIN DYNAMICS 365 FOR OPERATIONS
MODULE 1: CONFIGURING THE PRODUCT INFORMATION MANAGEMENT CONTROLS

Creating a Time based Unit

Now we will add a few more **Unit** records. Another unit that we want to track within the system is Hours, which is a **Time** based unit.

How to do it...

Step 1: Click New

So now we will add another **Unit** record.

Click on the **New** button.

Step 2: Update the Unit

Now that we have a new record we will want to assign an identifier for this Unit.

Set the **Unit** to **hr**

Step 3: Update the Description

Just like before we will want to add a more detailed description of the **Unit**.

Set the Description to Hour

Step 4: Select the Unit class

This **Unit** does not track the default **Quantity** though which is the default Unit class. This **Unit** is based on time.

So we will want to update the **Unit class** for this **Unit.**

Click on the **Unit class** dropdown list and select **Time**

Step 5: Update the Decimal precision

Also, hours are not discrete units of measure. We tend to track them down to the fraction of a unit.

By default the **Unit** record rounds to zero decimal places, but we will want to track this **Unit** to two decimal places.

So here we will want to change the **Decimal precision** for the **Unit.**

Set the Decimal precision to 2

DYNAMICS COMPANIONS
BARE BONES CONFIGURATION GUIDE

CONFIGURING PRODUCT INFORMATION MANAGEMENT WITHIN DYNAMICS 365 FOR OPERATIONS
MODULE 1: CONFIGURING THE PRODUCT INFORMATION MANAGEMENT CONTROLS

Creating a Time based Unit

How to do it...

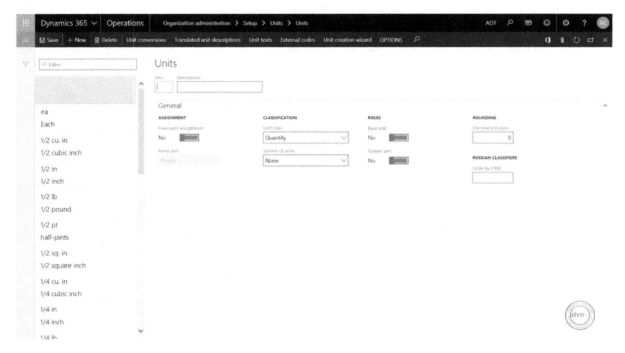

Step 1: Click New

So now we will add another **Unit** record.

To do this just click on the **New** button.

www.dynamicscompanions.com
Dynamics Companions

- 104 -

www.blindsquirrelpublishing.com
© 2017 Blind Squirrel Publishing, LLC , All Rights Reserved

BLIND SQUIRREL
PUBLISHING

DYNAMICS COMPANIONS
BARE BONES CONFIGURATION GUIDE

CONFIGURING PRODUCT INFORMATION MANAGEMENT WITHIN DYNAMICS 365 FOR OPERATIONS
MODULE 1: CONFIGURING THE PRODUCT INFORMATION MANAGEMENT CONTROLS

Creating a Time based Unit

How to do it...

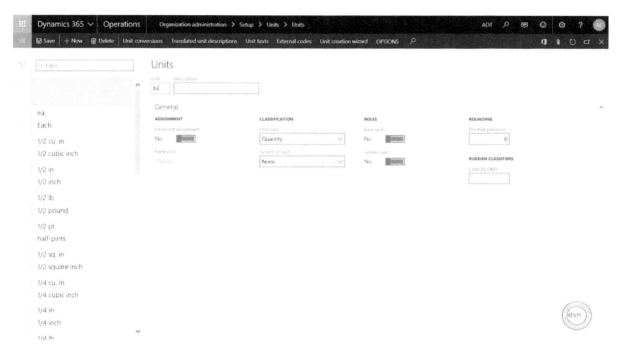

Step 2: Update the Unit

Now that we have a new record we will want to assign an identifier for this Unit.

To do this we will just need to type in the **Unit** value.

For this example, we will want to set the **Unit** to **hr**.

dyn

www.dynamicscompanions.com
Dynamics Companions

- 105 -

www.blindsquirrelpublishing.com
© 2017 Blind Squirrel Publishing, LLC , All Rights Reserved

BLIND SQUIRREL
PUBLISHING

DYNAMICS COMPANIONS
BARE BONES CONFIGURATION GUIDE

CONFIGURING PRODUCT INFORMATION MANAGEMENT WITHIN DYNAMICS 365 FOR OPERATIONS
MODULE 1: CONFIGURING THE PRODUCT INFORMATION MANAGEMENT CONTROLS

Creating a Time based Unit

How to do it...

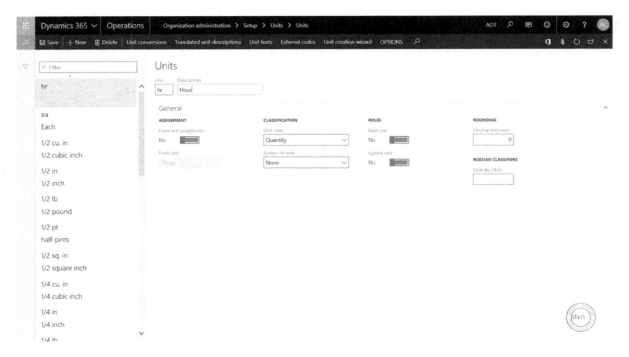

Step 3: Update the Description

Just like before we will want to add a more detailed description of the **Unit**.

To do this we will just need to update the **Description** value.

For this example, we will want to set the **Description** to **Hour**.

dync
www.dynamicscompanions.com
Dynamics Companions

- 106 -

www.blindsquirrelpublishing.com
© 2017 Blind Squirrel Publishing, LLC, All Rights Reserved

BLIND SQUIRREL
PUBLISHING

DYNAMICS COMPANIONS
BARE BONES CONFIGURATION GUIDE

CONFIGURING PRODUCT INFORMATION MANAGEMENT WITHIN DYNAMICS 365 FOR OPERATIONS
MODULE 1: CONFIGURING THE PRODUCT INFORMATION MANAGEMENT CONTROLS

Creating a Time based Unit

How to do it...

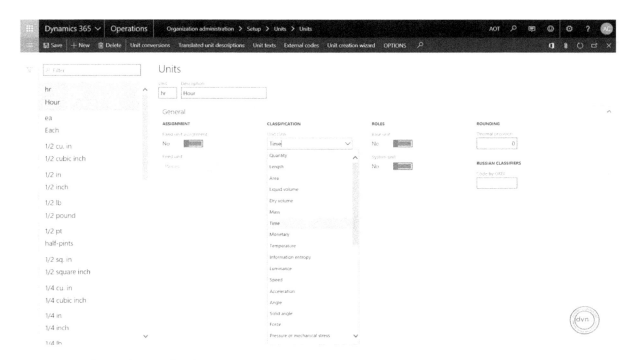

Step 4: Select the Unit class

This **Unit** does not track the default **Quantity** though which is the default Unit class. This **Unit** is based on time.

So we will want to update the **Unit class** for this **Unit.**

To do this we will just need to select the **Unit class** from the dropdown list.

For this Unit, we will want to click on the **Unit class** dropdown list and select **Time**.

dyn
www.dynamicscompanions.com
Dynamics Companions

- 107 -

www.blindsquirrelpublishing.com
© 2017 Blind Squirrel Publishing, LLC, All Rights Reserved

BLIND SQUIRREL
PUBLISHING

DYNAMICS COMPANIONS
BARE BONES CONFIGURATION GUIDE

CONFIGURING PRODUCT INFORMATION MANAGEMENT WITHIN DYNAMICS 365 FOR OPERATIONS
MODULE 1: CONFIGURING THE PRODUCT INFORMATION MANAGEMENT CONTROLS

Creating a Time based Unit

How to do it...

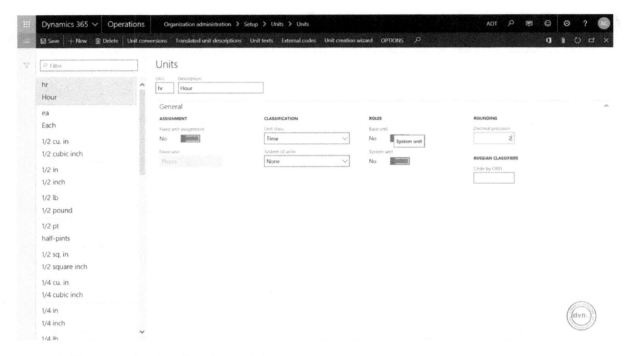

Step 5: Update the Decimal precision

Also, hours are not discrete units of measure. We tend to track them down to the fraction of a unit.

By default the **Unit** record rounds to zero decimal places, but we will want to track this **Unit** to two decimal places.

So here we will want to change the **Decimal precision** for the **Unit.**

To do this we will just need to update the **Decimal precision** value.

For this example, we will want to set the **Decimal precision** to **2**.

After we have done that we have set up our new **Unit**.

www.dynamicscompanions.com
Dynamics Companions

- 108 -

www.blindsquirrelpublishing.com
© 2017 Blind Squirrel Publishing, LLC , All Rights Reserved

BLIND SQUIRREL
PUBLISHING

DYNAMICS COMPANIONS
BARE BONES CONFIGURATION GUIDE

CONFIGURING PRODUCT INFORMATION MANAGEMENT WITHIN DYNAMICS 365 FOR OPERATIONS
MODULE 1: CONFIGURING THE PRODUCT INFORMATION MANAGEMENT CONTROLS

Creating an Electric Charge based Unit

Now we will add a final **Unit** record, which will allow us to track Ampere which we will need later on. We could track this as a quantity based unit, but for this one we will get a little fancier and use some of the more obscure Unit types.

How to do it...

Step 1: Click New

So now we will add one last **Unit** record.

Click on the **New** button.

Step 2: Update the Unit

Now that we have a new record we will want to assign an identifier for this Unit.

Set the **Unit** to **amps**

Step 3: Update the Description

And we will want to add a more detailed description of the **Unit**.

Set the Description to Ampage

Step 4: Select the Unit class

This **Unit** does not track the **Quantity** either. This **Unit** is based on electric charge.

So we will want to update the **Unit class** for this **Unit.**

Click on the **Unit class** dropdown list and select **Electric charge**

Step 5: Update the Decimal precision

Also, amps are not discrete units of measure. We will want to track them down to the fraction of a unit.

So here we will want to change the **Decimal precision** for the **Unit.**

Set the Decimal precision to 2

DYNAMICS COMPANIONS
BARE BONES CONFIGURATION GUIDE

CONFIGURING PRODUCT INFORMATION MANAGEMENT WITHIN DYNAMICS 365 FOR OPERATIONS
MODULE 1: CONFIGURING THE PRODUCT INFORMATION MANAGEMENT CONTROLS

Creating an Electric Charge based Unit

How to do it...

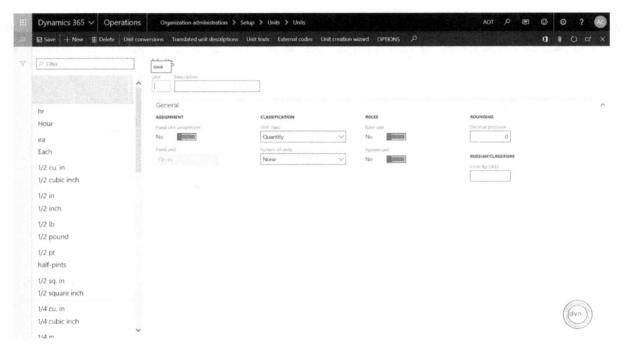

Step 1: Click New

So now we will add one last **Unit** record.

To do this just click on the **New** button.

www.dynamicscompanions.com
Dynamics Companions

- 110 -

www.blindsquirrelpublishing.com
© 2017 Blind Squirrel Publishing, LLC , All Rights Reserved

BLIND SQUIRREL
PUBLISHING

DYNAMICS COMPANIONS
BARE BONES CONFIGURATION GUIDE

CONFIGURING PRODUCT INFORMATION MANAGEMENT WITHIN DYNAMICS 365 FOR OPERATIONS
MODULE 1: CONFIGURING THE PRODUCT INFORMATION MANAGEMENT CONTROLS

Creating an Electric Charge based Unit

How to do it...

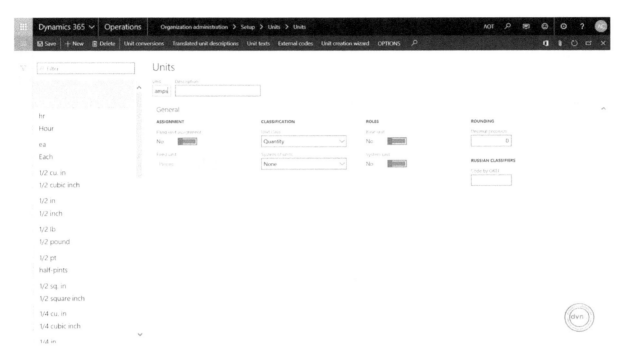

Step 2: Update the Unit

Now that we have a new record we will want to assign an identifier for this Unit.

To do this we will just need to update the **Unit** value.

For this example, we will want to set the **Unit** to **amps**.

www.dynamicscompanions.com
Dynamics Companions

- 111 -

www.blindsquirrelpublishing.com
© 2017 Blind Squirrel Publishing, LLC, All Rights Reserved

BLIND SQUIRREL
PUBLISHING

DYNAMICS COMPANIONS
BARE BONES CONFIGURATION GUIDE

CONFIGURING PRODUCT INFORMATION MANAGEMENT WITHIN DYNAMICS 365 FOR OPERATIONS
MODULE 1: CONFIGURING THE PRODUCT INFORMATION MANAGEMENT CONTROLS

Creating an Electric Charge based Unit

How to do it...

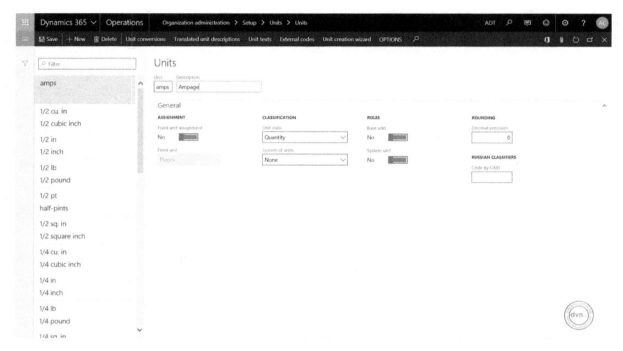

Step 3: Update the Description

And we will want to add a more detailed description of the **Unit**.

To do this we will just need to update the **Description** value.

For this example, we will want to set the **Description** to **Ampage**.

www.dynamicscompanions.com
Dynamics Companions

- 112 -

www.blindsquirrelpublishing.com
© 2017 Blind Squirrel Publishing, LLC , All Rights Reserved

BLIND SQUIRREL
PUBLISHING

DYNAMICS COMPANIONS
BARE BONES CONFIGURATION GUIDE

CONFIGURING PRODUCT INFORMATION MANAGEMENT WITHIN DYNAMICS 365 FOR OPERATIONS
MODULE 1: CONFIGURING THE PRODUCT INFORMATION MANAGEMENT CONTROLS

Creating an Electric Charge based Unit

How to do it...

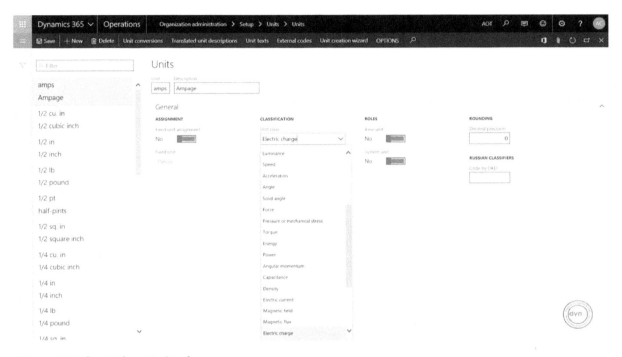

Step 4: Select the Unit class

This **Unit** does not track the **Quantity** either. This **Unit** is based on electric charge.

So we will want to update the **Unit class** for this **Unit**.

To do this we will just need to select the **Unit class** from the dropdown list.

For this example, we will want to click on the **Unit class** dropdown list and select **Electric charge**.

DYNAMICS COMPANIONS
BARE BONES CONFIGURATION GUIDE

CONFIGURING PRODUCT INFORMATION MANAGEMENT WITHIN DYNAMICS 365 FOR OPERATIONS
MODULE 1: CONFIGURING THE PRODUCT INFORMATION MANAGEMENT CONTROLS

Creating an Electric Charge based Unit

How to do it...

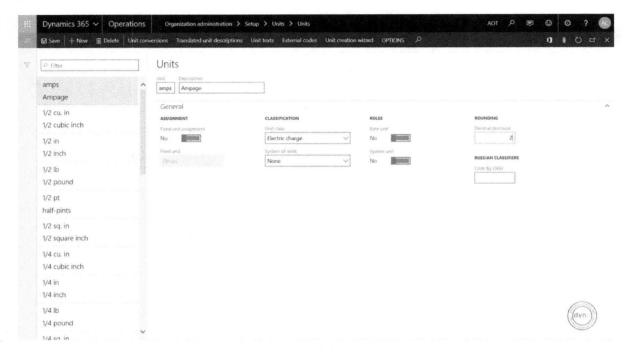

Step 5: Update the Decimal precision

Also, amps are not discrete units of measure. We will want to track them down to the fraction of a unit.

So here we will want to change the **Decimal precision** for the **Unit.**

To do this we will just need to update the **Decimal precision** value.

For this example, we will want to set the **Decimal precision** to **2**.

Once you have done that, click on the **Close** button to exit from the form.

www.dynamicscompanions.com
Dynamics Companions

- 114 -

www.blindsquirrelpublishing.com
© 2017 Blind Squirrel Publishing, LLC, All Rights Reserved

BLIND SQUIRREL
PUBLISHING

DYNAMICS COMPANIONS
BARE BONES CONFIGURATION GUIDE

CONFIGURING PRODUCT INFORMATION MANAGEMENT WITHIN DYNAMICS 365 FOR OPERATIONS
MODULE 1: CONFIGURING THE PRODUCT INFORMATION MANAGEMENT CONTROLS

Summary

Well done. You have now configured all of the main Units that we will be using later on within this module. Luckily we didn't have to set up all of the Units ourselves, the Wizard did most of the work for us. And even though we had to add a few more units on the fly, that wasn't a lot of work either.

DYNAMICS COMPANIONS
BARE BONES CONFIGURATION GUIDE

CONFIGURING PRODUCT INFORMATION MANAGEMENT WITHIN DYNAMICS 365 FOR OPERATIONS
MODULE 1: CONFIGURING THE PRODUCT INFORMATION MANAGEMENT CONTROLS

Review

Congratulations. We have now finished the all of the base configuration that we need for the Product Information Management. We can now move on to more exciting things like the creation of new Products within the system.

DYNAMICS COMPANIONS
BARE BONES CONFIGURATION GUIDE

CONFIGURING PRODUCT INFORMATION MANAGEMENT WITHIN DYNAMICS 365 FOR OPERATIONS
MODULE 1: CONFIGURING THE PRODUCT INFORMATION MANAGEMENT CONTROLS

About The Author

Murray Fife is an Author of over 20 books on Microsoft Dynamics including the Bare Bones Configuration Guide series. These guides comprise of over 15 books which step you through the setup and configuration of Microsoft Dynamics including Finance, Operations, Human Resources, Production, Service Management, and Project Accounting.

Throughout his 25+ years of experience in the software industry he has worked in many different roles during his career, including as a developer, an implementation consultant, a trainer and a demo guy within the partner channel which gives him a great understanding of the requirements for both customers and partners perspective.

If you are interested in contacting Murray or want to follow his blogs and posts then here is all of his contact information:

Email: murray@murrayfife.com

Twitter: @murrayfife
Facebook: facebook.com/murraycfife
Google: google.com/+murrayfife
LinkedIn: linkedin.com/in/murrayfife

Blog: atinkerersnotebook.com
Slideshare: slideshare.net/murrayfife
Amazon: amazon.com/author/murrayfife

www.dynamicscompanions.com
Dynamics Companions

- 117 -

www.blindsquirrelpublishing.com
© 2017 Blind Squirrel Publishing, LLC , All Rights Reserved

BLIND SQUIRREL
PUBLISHING

DYNAMICS COMPANIONS
BARE BONES CONFIGURATION GUIDE

CONFIGURING PRODUCT INFORMATION MANAGEMENT WITHIN DYNAMICS 365 FOR OPERATIONS
MODULE 1: CONFIGURING THE PRODUCT INFORMATION MANAGEMENT CONTROLS

Need More Help with Microsoft Dynamics AX 2012 or Dynamics 365 for Operations

We are firm believers that Microsoft Dynamics AX 2012 or Dynamics 365 is not a hard product to learn, but the problem is where do you start. Which is why we developed the Bare Bones Configuration Guides. The aim of this series is to step you though the configuration of Microsoft Dynamics from a blank system, and then step you through the setup of all of the core modules within Microsoft Dynamics. We start with the setup of a base system, then move on to the financial, distribution, and operations modules.

Each book builds upon the previous ones, and by the time you have worked through all of the guides then you will have completely configured a simple (but functional) Microsoft Dynamics instance. To make it even more worthwhile you will have a far better understanding of Microsoft Dynamics and also how everything fits together.

As of now there are 16 guides in this series broken out as follows:

- Configuring a Training Environment
- Configuring an Organization
- Configuring the General Ledger
- Configuring Cash and Bank Management
- Configuring Accounts Receivable
- Configuring Accounts Payable
- Configuring Product Information Management
- Configuring Inventory Management

- Configuring Procurement and Sourcing
- Configuring Sales Order Management
- Configuring Human Resource Management
- Configuring Project Management and Accounting
- Configuring Production Control
- Configuring Sales and Marketing
- Configuring Service Management
- Configuring Warehouse Management

Although you can get each of these guides individually, and we think that each one is a great Visual resources to step you through each of the particular modules, for those of you that want to take full advantage of the series, you will want to start from the beginning and work through them one by one. After you have done that you would have done people told me was impossible for one persons to do, and that is to configure all of the core modules within Microsoft Dynamics.

If you are interested in finding out more about the series and also view all of the details including topics covered within the module, then browse to the Bare Bones Configuration Guide landing page on the Microsoft Dynamics Companions website. You will find all of the details, and also downloadable resources that help you with the setup of Microsoft Dynamics. Here is the full link: http://www.dynamicscompanions.com/

dyn   www.dynamicscompanions.com
      Dynamics Companions

- 119 -

www.blindsquirrelpublishing.com
© 2017 Blind Squirrel Publishing, LLC, All Rights Reserved

BLIND SQUIRREL
PUBLISHING

DYNAMICS COMPANIONS
BARE BONES CONFIGURATION GUIDE

CONFIGURING PRODUCT INFORMATION MANAGEMENT WITHIN DYNAMICS 365 FOR OPERATIONS
MODULE 1: CONFIGURING THE PRODUCT INFORMATION MANAGEMENT CONTROLS

Usage Agreement

Blind Squirrel Publishing, LLC (the Publisher) agrees to grant, and the user of the eBook agrees to accept, a nonexclusive license to use the eBook under the terms and conditions of this eBook License Agreement ("Agreement"). Your use of the eBook constitutes your agreement to the terms and conditions set forth in this Agreement. This Agreement, or any part thereof, cannot be changed, waived, or discharged other than by a statement in writing signed by you and Blind Squirrel Publishing, LLC. Please read the entire Agreement carefully.

EBook Usage. The eBook may be used by one user on any device. The user of the eBook shall be subject to all of the terms of this Agreement, whether or not the user was the purchaser.

Printing. You may occasionally print a few pages of the text (but not entire sections), which may include sending the printed pages to a third party in the normal course of your business, but you must warn the recipient in writing that copyright law prohibits the recipient from redistributing the eBook content to anyone else. Other than the above, you may not print pages and/or distribute eBook content to others.

Copyright, Use and Resale Prohibitions. The Publisher retains all rights not expressly granted to you in this Agreement. The software, content, and related documentation in the eBook are protected by copyright laws and international copyright treaties, as well as other intellectual property laws and treaties. Nothing in this Agreement constitutes a waiver of the publisher's rights. The Publisher will not be responsible for performance problems due to circumstances beyond its reasonable control. Other than as stated in this Agreement, you may not copy, print, modify, remove, delete, augment, add to, publish, transmit, sell, resell, license, create derivative works from, or in any way exploit any of the eBook's content, in whole or in part, in print or electronic form, and you may not aid or permit others to do so. The unauthorized use or distribution of copyrighted or other proprietary content is illegal and could subject the purchaser to substantial damages. Purchaser will be liable for any damage resulting from any violation of this Agreement.

No Transfer. This license is not transferable by the eBook purchaser unless such transfer is approved in advance by the Publisher.

Disclaimer. The eBook, or any support given by the Publisher are in no way substitutes for assistance from legal, tax, accounting, or other qualified professionals. If legal advice or other expert assistance is required, the services of a competent professional person should be sought.

Limitation of Liability. The eBook is provided "as is" and the Publisher does not make any warranty or representation, either express or implied, to the eBook, including its quality, accuracy, performance, merchantability, or fitness for a particular purpose. You assume the entire risk as to the results and performance of the eBook. The Publisher does not warrant, guarantee, or make any representations regarding the use of, or the results obtained with, the eBook in terms of accuracy, correctness or reliability. In no event will the Publisher be liable for indirect, special, incidental, or consequential damages arising out of delays, errors, omissions, inaccuracies, or the use or inability to use the eBook, or for interruption of the eBook, from whatever cause. This will apply even if the Publisher has been advised that the possibility of such damage exists. Specifically, the Publisher is not responsible for any costs, including those incurred as a result of lost profits or revenue, loss of data, the cost of recovering such programs or data, the cost of any substitute program, claims by third parties, or similar costs. Except for the Publisher's indemnification obligations in Section 7.2, in no case will the Publisher's liability exceed the amount of license fees paid.

www.dynamicscompanions.com
Dynamics Companions

- 121 -

DYNAMICS COMPANIONS
BARE BONES CONFIGURATION GUIDE

CONFIGURING PRODUCT INFORMATION MANAGEMENT WITHIN DYNAMICS 365 FOR OPERATIONS
MODULE 1: CONFIGURING THE PRODUCT INFORMATION MANAGEMENT CONTROLS

Hold Harmless / Indemnification.

7.1 You agree to defend, indemnify and hold the Publisher and any third party provider harmless from and against all third party claims and damages (including reasonable attorneys' fees) regarding your use of the eBook, unless the claims or damages are due to the Publisher's or any third party provider's gross negligence or willful misconduct or arise out of an allegation for which the Publisher is obligated to indemnify you.

7.The Publisher shall defend, indemnify and hold you harmless at the Publisher's expense in any suit, claim or proceeding brought against you alleging that your use of the eBook delivered to you hereunder directly infringes a United States patent, copyright, trademark, trade secret, or other third party proprietary right, provided the Publisher is (i) promptly notified, (ii) given the assistance required at the Publisher's expense, and (iii) permitted to retain legal counsel of the Publisher's choice and to direct the defense. The Publisher also agrees to pay any damages and costs awarded against you by final judgment of a court of last resort in any such suit or any agreed settlement amount on account of any such alleged infringement, but the Publisher will have no liability for settlements or costs incurred without its consent. Should your use of any such eBook be enjoined, or in the event that the Publisher desires to minimize its liability hereunder, the Publisher will, at its option and expense, (i) substitute a fully equivalent non-infringing eBook for the infringing item; (ii) modify the infringing item so that it no longer infringes but remains substantially equivalent; or (iii) obtain for you the right to continue use of such item. If none of the foregoing is feasible, the Publisher will terminate your access to the eBook and refund to you the applicable fees paid by you for the infringing item(s). THE FOREGOING STATES THE ENTIRE LIABILITY OF THE PUBLISHER AND YOUR SOLE REMEDY FOR INFRINGEMENT OR FOR ANY BREACH OF WARRANTY OF NON-INFRINGEMENT, EXPRESS OR IMPLIED. THIS INDEMNITY WILL NOT APPLY TO ANY ALLEGED INFRINGEMENT BASED UPON A COMBINATION OF OTHER SOFTWARE OR INFORMATION WITH THE EBOOK WHERE THE EBOOK WOULD NOT HAVE OTHERWISE INFRINGED ON ITS OWN.